Tim Hayward

Big Green Egg

FEASTS

Innovative Recipes to Cook for Friends and Family

Managing Director
Sarah Lavelle

Project Editor
Sophie Allen

Head of Design
Claire Rochford

Designer
Nikki Ellis

Photographer
Sam Folan

Props Stylist
Faye Wears

Food Stylist
Joss Herd

Recipe Developer
Matt Williamson

Production Director
Stephen Lang

Production Controller
Gary Hayes

Published in 2023 by Quadrille,
an imprint of Hardie Grant Publishing

Quadrille
52–54 Southwark Street
London SE1 1UN
quadrille.com

Cataloguing in Publication Data: a
catalogue record for this book is available
from the British Library.

Text © Tim Hayward 2023
Photography © Sam Folan 2023
Design © Quadrille 2023

ISBN 978 1 78713 906 0

Printed in China

CONTENTS

INTRODUCTION

Over recent years we've taken great strides forward in cooking, both indoors and out, and our approach to barbecues and grills has become a lot more nuanced. Funny, isn't it? We used to speak about having a 'barbie' in the garden and it was all simple – but now every backyard tong-jockey worth his comedy apron can talk for hours on the authentic 'cue traditions of various Southern States, and half the restaurants in town are grilling on live fire. Somehow a wire grating and some petrol-soaked briquettes no longer cut the mustard.

For me, this is where the excitement of the Big Green Egg begins. When it first arrived, it might have felt like a prestige garden barbie, but as our knowledge of fire cooking has developed and the range of customizations and specialized kit has expanded, it's become the essential tool kit for the inquisitive and adventurous food enthusiast. Sure, you can 'barbecue' on an EGG – in fact you can configure it to pretty much replicate a down-home slow-roasting pit – but you can also set it up for a North Eastern crab boil or to supply the searing heat for authentic wok cooking. With accessories (and occasionally, ingenuity) you can create the tiny, controllable grilling environments of a mangal or a yakitori ya. All of our food enthusiasms are met when we can set it up as a live-fire oven for our handmade sourdoughs, a creditable tandoor or a 'forno' that can reach the temperatures demanded by pizzas.

It's interesting to consider when we, particularly in the UK, lost connection with our food traditions, but some social historians have reckoned that, as we went through the Industrial Revolution, more and more people moved to cities to work in factories. Detached from their agricultural roots, they learned to cook in the tiny kitchens of their urban homes, in themselves 'industrialized' spaces with increasingly 'clean' and efficient sources of heat and water.

Other cultures have industrialised at different speeds and not all have become as deracinated as we have. Coupled with the internet, which gives us immediate access to communities of cooks and seemingly unlimited recipes, the versatility of the EGG gives us the ability to recreate all kinds of cooking experiences at will. It's a multiplier of culinary learning. For me, every act of replicating these phenomenal food traditions teaches me something new... perhaps something lost... about heat and ingredients – a deeper knowledge which makes me a better, more considered cook.

But there's something else, arguably something more important that we can learn from the diversity of culinary traditions with which we're experimenting. As well as losing our connection with fire and ingredients, we miss an incredibly important facet of eating. We seem to have lost our ability to feast.

Today, food supply and packaging are so efficient that almost everyone has choice in what they eat. We increasingly eat different things at different times and, rather than sitting down together as family or friends, to 'break bread' and socialise, we take our own favourite foods into metaphorical corners to eat alone. This unfortunate, literally 'antisocial' eating behaviour is quietly spreading right across the world. It may not be too late to stop it and, if there's an antidote, it's almost certainly more feasting.

Christmas and Thanksgiving seem to have remained reasonably successful as occasions to get together and eat, but that's a pretty weak offering. It's true that, with modern families often geographically fragmented, it's difficult to get everyone in the same place for, say, a weekly Sabbath meal, but shouldn't that just encourage us to make a little more effort on the occasions when we can assemble?

One of the unexpected advantages of the Big Green Egg is its totemic appearance and kind of hulking mass. The way it forms a physical centre to a gathering, a sort of warm, green heart, is entirely unique. Just setting it up puts you halfway to a feast, and a great way to complete the job is to respectfully cook things that honour feasting cultures and that encourage the very best sort of social eating.

This book tries to bring together these two ideas in a series of feasts, for groups of all sizes, which are rooted in experimental cooking and social eating. We take the unique advantages of the Big Green Egg as a massively versatile cooking device, adaptable to almost any culinary tradition, and create dishes around which we can build occasions. Each section can be served as a single grand feast or you can cherry pick and chop and change the dishes that appeal to you most. Some recipes are for large, sharing dishes that constitute a feast in themselves, some are for dishes that will form a centrepiece to feasts of your own devising. Some, we hope, will stimulate your own experiments, but, hopefully, every recipe will impart new tricks and techniques, build your confidence as a cook and add new favourites to your repertoire.

At the beginning of each feast, we've given you some help with your preparations. Alongside the full Feast Menu, you'll find an EGG Feast Set Up.

This is the way you'll need to set up your EGG ahead of cooking and how you might need to change things during the cook. Read this because altering hot kit 'on-the-fly' is probably the toughest part of working with the EGG and, as with anything else, preparedness is everything.

You'll also find a Feast Method. This is the running order for cooking the feast, broadly laying out the sequence of the different phases of each recipe to bring the whole lot to the table at once. Once again, read it through several times before you start.

THE EGG AND EGGSESSORIES

INDIRECT SET-UP
Indirect set-up works like a convection oven. By blocking the fire's direct heat with a convEGGtor, you take away its intensity. This gives an even heat that deflects around the dome of the EGG. It provides the perfect cooking conditions for roasting, cooking low and slow and smoking.

DIRECT SET-UP
What most people recognize as traditional barbecuing, in direct set-up the heat of the charcoal has direct contact with the food you are cooking. This means tasty, caramelized charlines and a distinct, smokey umami flavour.

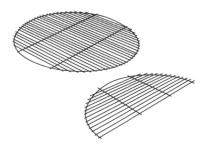

STAINLESS STEEL GRID
This is the basic grid, standard to most outdoor grills. It's a good general purpose surface - easy to keep clean and less likely to stick or scorch than cast-iron.

In half moon configuration, you can combine it as part of the EGGspander system.

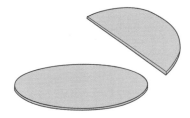

BAKING STONE
Turn your EGG into a perfect pizza oven with the simple addition of a baking stone. Pulling moisture from the outer surface of the dough and distributing the heat evenly, you'll produce delicious breads and bakes. To maximize on space, as part of the EGGspander system, use the half moon baking stone to easily whip up some flatbreads while you're grilling the main event.

DIRTY
Cooking on your EGG in the most basic form allows the high-quailty lumpwood charcoal to give an intense, elemental flavour to your food.

PLANCHA

With a dual-sided design, the Big Green Egg plancha is the perfect surface for sautéing vegetables, and for searing meat and fish. Authentic, high temperature grilling is made quick and easy with this great piece of kit.

CAST-IRON GRID

For perfect sear marks and amazing heat retention, look no further than the cast-iron grid. The half moon version is part of the EGGspander system.

SKILLETS AND PANS

Searing, braising, baking, sautéing or roasting – the Big Green Egg cast-iron skillet or paella pan is one of the most versatile pieces of kit you can own.

CONVEGGTOR®

A key accessory for all Big Green Egg owners, this clever ceramic insert turns your EGG into a convection oven, for baking, slow-cooking, smoking, and roasting. The three-legged design stimulates heat circulation around the EGG without exposing food to the direct heat of the fire burning below.

DUTCH OVEN

Offering efficient heat distribution and excellent durability, the Big Green Egg cast-iron Dutch oven is an essential addition to your collection. A favourite for soups, stews and curries.

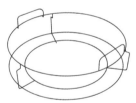

CONVEGGTOR BASKET

The ConvEGGtor basket is the base of the EGGspander system and is designed to hold the ceramic ConvEGGtor and gives it handles to make it easier to lift in and out of the EGG (use gloves when hot). With or without the ConvEGGtor, it raises your main cooking surface until it's flush with the rim of the EGG and also enables you to use a half moon baking stone instead of the ConvEGGtor to create a half direct/indirect setup.

WOK

Ideal for stir fries - but a great everyday pan for frying, poaching, braising, roasting and baking.

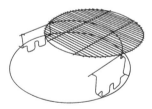

MULTI-LEVEL RACK FOR EGGSPANDER

This fits on top of the convEGGtor basket and your first level of cooking surfaces. There is a handy sliding top shelf made of stainless steel or you can use Big Green Egg surfaces of the next size down for even more options.

PLACEMENT OF YOUR EGG

I'm going to freely admit to being a huge food nerd who's constantly experimenting. I know a lot of people love the EGG for its 'straight-out-of-the box' simplicity – just spark up and cook – but it's the incredible versatility that does it for me. I get so excited by interesting cuisines and techniques from all around the world and now, thanks to the madness of the internet, recipes and ingredients are available to us, so the EGG – and its ability to be configured as anything from a Polynesian cooking pit to a Tunisian clay bread oven – has become my best mate, my sandbox and my research lab.

I'm lucky to live in a place where the kitchen has large sliding doors onto a terrace garden. It means that, except on the most Baltic of days, I can slide open a door and the EGG is effectively part of my kitchen. When I'm entertaining or when we're eating outside as a family, I also have all the facilities of the kitchen just a pace

away. This is obviously not possible for everyone but it's worth bearing in mind when you consider how your EGG is going to be sited. If you're part of the new generation of outdoor cooks, who are building more comprehensive outdoor kitchens – with sinks and fridges – all I can say is I'm very jealous, and you can build as far away from the house as you'd like. For me, nearer the kitchen is good.

But this isn't just about having to traipse across the lawn with groaning platters of raw meat. I'm an absolute believer in integrating the EGG into day-to-day cooking so, while there may be, say, a dozen occasions per year when I cater for twenty over a sprawling afternoon of eating and drinking, there are dozens more occasions when I throw on a coat, slip outside and grill a couple of pieces of fish for dinner. Set up your EGG where you can use it most conveniently and most often.

THE EGGSPANDER SYSTEM

An EGG's potential to produce spectacular multi-dish feasts, from Sunday roasts to Spanish tapas, has been transformed by the game-changing arrival of the EGGspander. This innovative system significantly increases your EGG's capacity and allows for the simultaneous use of different surfaces and cooking modes.

With almost limitless configurations, the EGGspander enables you to grill meat in one zone, whilst roasting your potatoes in another, leaving your gravy to bubble away above. If you're new to the EGG, it's THE indispensable accessory to go for. If you're not, you're going to wonder how you survived without it.

STEP 1: ADD THE CONVEGGTOR BASKET
The convEGGtor basket is the housing for your EGGspander System. It consists of a frame that will essentially provide two levels for surfaces; an upper and a lower. If you are not cooking a whole EGGspander feast, it is a handy piece of equipment to hold your convEGGtor when cooking indirectly for roasts and low and slow.

STEP 2: ADD YOUR HALF MOON SURFACES
Place your convEGGtor basket next to your EGG, so you can build a basic formation. Insert the half moon cast-iron searing grid on the upper left of the convEGGtor basket, the half moon baking stone lower right and the half moon stainless steel grid upper right. This will allow you to cook directly on one side of the EGG and indirectly on the other.

STEP 3: ADD YOUR MULTI-LEVEL RACK
For even greater cooking space and better organisation, add the multi-level rack to the convEGGtor basket. Fantastic at warming an entire feast through. This step is optional.

The EGGspander is engineered to fit in the Large and XL models, so if you're working with a MiniMax, now may be the time to grow your EGG family.

LIGHTING AND USING

The EGG also represents some of the oldest technology we humans have – pretty much since discovering fire, we've been learning to contain and direct it. The EGG, very simply, creates a safe and contained space for burning fuel, ways to control the airflow to it, ways to support food over it and ways to enclose and direct the heat.

And what excites me is the massive freedom that affords the cook.

The first thing that surprises traditional grill users when they first encounter the EGG is the rather different relationship you have with the fuel. I kind of 'fill up' the EGG, much like I would my car, whenever it needs it. My XL takes maybe half a bag of Big Green Egg charcoal. It takes around 15 minutes to light and bring up to temperature, depending on what you are going to cook. I do my cooking then to turn it off, I

close the vents and the dome. It's all ready to light again, the second I need it and I may do two or three moderate cooking sessions on it before I need to 'refuel'. It's a very different and considerably more clean and convenient way of approaching things.

To light the EGG, I lift the lid and take a look at the charcoal. If it's been used once before, it's a good idea to rake through thoroughly, mixing the partially burnt in with the untouched and giving any ash the chance to drop through the bottom grating where it can be raked out in a few seconds. Unlike a regular garden grill, you're not going to need a charcoal chimney, half a gallon of meths or a blowtorch. It turns out the best way to get charcoal alight is with several gentle little flames, burning quite slowly. You'll need the kind of firestarters that are made of some soft

organic material, like wood shavings or dust, bound with wax… almost like little wickless candles (Big Green Egg do their own excellent version of premium natural firelighters).

Break off a firestarter and place in the middle of the EGG on top of the charcoal. MiniMax, Large and XL take a single firestarter; if you're cooking pizza or steaks on an XL I would recommend two. Light each one gently with a match or lighter – no need for that flamethrower – and then pile one or two pieces of charcoal over each little conflagration, with both vents and the dome wide open, leaving plenty of space for airflow. I know it's weird but I can't tell you how much I love this process. It's very contemplative and nurturing. I usually leave the lid up for 10 minutes or until the fire starter has burned away.

You'll need to check with your recipe whether you're going to be wanting direct or indirect heat. If it's indirect, a general rule of thumb is that you should add your convEGGtor or cooking surfaces at a 20°C/70°F lower temperature than your EGG target temperature, bar pizza or high temperature grilling. The EGGspander convEGGtor basket makes it easy to place the convEGGtor and, uniquely, makes it simple to lift it out again during cooking if you wish. You can also create a half indirect zone by using the half moon baking stone in the convEGGtor basket in place of the convEGGtor.

Next, you'll need to decide on your cooking surfaces, from which there's a wide range and myriad combinations. Choose whether you want a single grill, be it stainless steel or cast-iron, a plancha or stone – or use half surfaces to create a combination. With the upper part of the EGGspander System, the 2 Piece Multi Level Rack, you can now also create a second, higher cooking layer.

With all this assembled and in position, close the dome, keep the vents open, and let the EGG begin to rise to temperature.

'BURPING' THE EGG

Cooking with the dome down means you will need to open the dome with caution, especially when cooking at high temperatures. 'Burping' your EGG allows air to slowly and safely enter the dome, preventing any flare-ups that could cause a flash of heat to burn your hand.

First, open your dome a few centimetres/an inch, slowly and carefully.

Bounce the lid slightly for a few seconds. This will allow smoke and heat to escape and oxygen to enter gradually, so you avoid a backdraft.

It will now be safe to open the dome fully. You'll need to burp your EGG every time you open it.

For more information on loading and lighting and other helpful tips, please see the Guides section on the website.

FUEL

Let's consider the fuel for a moment. I have to confess to being more than a little obsessed with it. Charcoal's just such a fascinating material. With the good, artisanally made stuff, wood is cut and carefully stacked, then covered with layers of soil and damp cloth to make a controllable airtight container – in a rather entertaining way, it's much like the EGG itself. The wood is then lit, then the charcoal burner will control vents at the bottom of the stack and an exhaust hole at the top, so that the wood has enough oxygen to 'pyrolize' or char, but not to burst into flames. It's an incredibly elegant bit of science. The wood sort of 'cooks', changing its chemical composition, turning slowly from a mixture of cellulose, lignin, water and a bunch of other organic compounds, into pure carbon. All the impurities, the volatile compounds, the moisture, the tars and oils are burned clear away.

We know we can trust good reliable heat and control it through airflow, but we also know that flavours are only created by a) impurities that drip onto the fire from the food… fat, juices and marinades, b) flavours we add to the fire, like smoking chips, or c) using the heat to change the chemical composition of the food by caramelization or charring (also known as the Maillard reaction) and, d) the type of hardwood lumpwood charcoal that you use. The reason we buy quality charcoal is for its purity and the quality and provenance of its manufacture.

In a set-up like the EGG, which is all about the maximum efficiency of burning and careful fuel management, it's a false economy to buy cheap charcoal. It doesn't necessarily have to be 'hand-made' – some of the very best is made in kilns rather than rustic 'stacks', but it mustn't be incompletely burned, in small dusty pieces as much cheap charcoal is, or, God forbid, in 'briquettes' made of charcoal dust, recompressed and often with added binders. All of these will burn inefficiently, add unpleasant flavours and fill your Big Green Egg with dust and ash.

The good stuff comes in big chunks, is sustainably harvested and produced and burns hot and clean; it'll cost you more than the cheap nonsense but you'll burn half as much. Big Green Egg's charcoal is lumpwood, and all made from hardwood. Hardwood is better at burning than softwood because it gives you a consistent, longer, hotter burn. Typical hardwoods are oak, hickory, maple and eucalyptus.

I'm sure I don't need to say this but, if you buy charcoal that's packed in paraffin soaked bags or impregnated with accelerants to make it 'easy to light', then you deserve sausages that taste like a burned-out car and it might be better to consider a tinfoil grill from a gas station and donating your EGG to someone who deserves it.

TOOLS AND EQUIPMENT

You can run your EGG straight out of the box with very little extra equipment, but over time you'll build up a little collection of kit so it's worth putting some thought into what's actually necessary. It's too easy to clutter up your workspace with bits, bobs and gadgetry so I always run by three very basic rules.

Rule 1: Only have kit you actually need. Space is limited at a busy grill station and something that isn't essential is a liability. Keep it simple.

Rule 2: Buy a cheap piece of kit and you will have a moment of satisfaction when you look at the receipt. Then you will use it. Every time you use it, you will curse its inadequacy until the day it breaks, at an incredibly inconvenient time. It's a simple equation. Poor kit buys you misery.

Good kit is usually expensive but it's worth the money. Every time you use it, you will feel a little burst of pleasure and it will probably last forever. Good kit buys you pleasure.

Rule 3: Buy a digital probe thermometer (see Rule 2) and use it obsessively.

Now let's work through in the order you're going to need things.

SET UP KIT

First of all, the physical wrangling kit. The stuff you need to get your EGG set up and working. I work on a small terrace so, for me, a wheeled support cage means I can shift things around and keep them out of the way when not in use. If you're lucky enough to have a static rig set-up, this won't be necessary. You're going to be doing a lot of work close to the EGG so you'll need to think about bench space. This will need to be easy to wipe clean, resistant to burning from hot equipment coming straight off the grill and – trust me, when you're my age, this is the most important thing – set at a safe working height to protect your back.

The standard height for a standing workstation is 880-900mm, which is conveniently where the range of Big Green Egg nests and tables will place your cooking and working surfaces. I personally favour the stainless-steel top of the modular Nest but the acacia shelves that can clip onto the sides of the EGG and neatly fold down and out of the way, can be a functional space saver if you have to share your prized outdoor kitchen space with such wasteful accessories as plants, pets or children.

The EGG produces very little ash so you probably won't need a separate ash-bin as you might with other types of barbecue. I've repurposed my metal bin to store my charcoal and keep it completely dry. You will though, grow to love the ash tool that comes with your EGG. It is, of course, beautifully designed for it's original purpose of taking the ash out of the bottom draft-door, but I don't know an EGG user anywhere who doesn't press it into service for everything. It can hook in and move a hot grid if you have to, and I know I'm not too proud to use it to shift food or pots on the grill when necessary. I'm still finding new uses for the ash tool but I'm pretty convinced that if I ever lose my arm in some terrible steak-eating accident, I'm going to get it replaced with a clip-on ash tool, like a grill-crazed Captain Hook.

Of course the real tool for moving grills and gratings, particularly when they're hot, is the grid lifter. This fascinates every guest who ever watches you grill and I sometimes think it is worth it just for that, but now the EGGspander System is with us (see page 11) there are fewer reasons to use it.

Traditionally pitmasters used to favour welders' gauntlets, great big coarse leather things that stopped you getting burned but robbed you of any dexterity. I remember when I first discovered Nomex gloves, you had to find places on the internet that sold them to fighter pilots, racing drivers and Formula 1 pit crews. People would laugh at you, cooking in 'woolly gloves'... until you did your party piece of picking up a hot coal or a searing hot metal grill. You can pick them up in most kitchen or outdoors stores now, but the EGG version is particularly well designed in a sober black, covering a lot of your forearm and equipped with little patches of non-slip material for when the fats really start flowing.

One word of warning. Make sure your gloves and your hands are scrupulously dry before handling anything hot. Moisture robs any cloth of its power to protect as water turns to steam – which can be even more damaging to skin than dry heat. Gloves allow you dexterity but are difficult to drop if you start getting steamed. Never handle anything hot with damp hands or gloves.

UTENSILS

Big Green Egg, as you might expect, make an excellent range of utensils, but these are the things that are most down to personal taste, so if you have something in your kitchen that you're happy working with, or if you're lucky enough to have found something beautiful made for you by a blacksmith, all well and good. You will need good tongs. This is important. They need to be long but it's absolutely vital that they don't twist.

There's a special place in hell for the manufacturers of twisty tongs, and it's well deserved. Whether you're approaching the tong stand at your local cookshop or you're discussing a bespoke pair with your personal tong-monger, pick up the tongs and grip something substantial in them. With your spare hand, try to pull the item out. It probably won't move... that's good. Now twist it. If you twist what they're holding and it pops out of the tongs, hurl them from you with great force, protesting loudly that you'll have no truck with them at all. Storm out. These are NOT the tongs you are looking for!

Most 'sets' of barbecue tools contain a long fork, which makes a certain kind of sense, but personally, I don't have much time for them. Most of the food I want to cook doesn't appreciate being repeatedly stabbed. It enables big pieces of meat, fish or vegetable to waste precious juices into the flames. I prefer to use tongs, a long-handled spatula – often assisted by the ash tool – or a smaller, standard kitchen fork, held in a hand protected by a glove.

Buy a full set, by all means, but you'll usually find you end up using just a couple of favourite hand tools and the rest can be left cluttering up the kitchen drawer.

SURFACES

The EGG is distinguished by its excellent variety of cooking surfaces which have now been multiplied in their permutations, by the EGGspander System.

To understand cooking surfaces, it's worth thinking a little about the physics of cooking. If you want to expose raw food to direct flame, to take advantage of a fast flow of 'convection' heat – the hot air that circulates in a closed space – you'll need a support structure that holds things firmly in place but doesn't get in the way. The simple, stainless-steel grid is ideal for this. It's light, conducts heat extremely well, is easy to clean and naturally quite non-stick. It doesn't 'hold' heat, but it's very good at holding things in heat.

A cast-iron plate or 'plancha' won't let the flame touch the food, but what it will do is build up heat of its own. It holds heat beautifully and will sear and char where it's in contact with the food. Whether that surface is smooth or ridged is rather a matter of aesthetics.

A cast-iron grid combines elements of both surfaces. It lets the flame through to sear food where it can, it contains heat and sears and cooks where it touches and, unlike the plancha, it allows a full flow of air around itself.

Finally, we have baking stones, which not only protect from flame but soak up enormous amounts of heat energy themselves, which they can then transmit back into the food at a slower rate. It's difficult to 'burn' food on a baking stone, but it will also output an incredibly regular heat for an enormous length of time. Baking stones are best for baking pizzas or breads and are really good under a cast-iron pot or pan. Real EGG pros know that a stone is so good at sucking up heat that they can be used to quickly drop the temperature. In an emergency, you can almost close the shutters on your EGG, put in a cold baking stone and in a few minutes the stone will be hot while the EGG temperature will have dropped tens of degrees. And always remember to burp your EGG when operating at hot temperatures.

VESSELS

Regular domestic pots, pans, cooking trays and casseroles work well in the EGG but there are one or two specialized pieces you might want to consider. EGG manufacture a baking stone with raised sides, which makes a uniquely good job of deep dish pizzas and fruit pies. You can achieve similar effects with a Spanish/South American 'cazuela' – a ceramic vessel that stores heat as well as transmits it.

Spanish paella pans are made of quite light-grade steel so dry food may stick to their bases, but they are really good for cooking liquid-based stews, braises and rice dishes. The wide surface area enables liquid to evaporate faster, thickening sauces quickly, and exposes more food to the overhead heat of the closed lid, so it can brown and crisp. Big Green Egg manufacture their own paella dishes with an enamel coating, which makes them a little less 'sticky', and prettier on the table.

There are plenty of cast-iron skillets on the market, including a couple of excellent ones from Big Green Egg, that are really the workhorses of fire cooking. They have some of the advantages of the paella dish – heat transmission and large surface areas – plus the heat 'holding' of the ceramic dishes, and the ability to brown and sear food.

It's worth seeking out a ceramic pot or casserole, which enables enclosed, indirect heat cooking in a vessel that holds and regularises heat. These occur in many cooking traditions; my own favourite is the Japanese 'donabe' but there are also excellent Chinese 'clay pots' and of course the Big Green Egg enamelled Dutch oven.

STORAGE/MISE EN PLACE

You'll need a system for storing and holding components and ingredients, keeping track of them and moving them seamlessly to-and-from your grill set-up. There are excellent plastic box systems with clip-on lids, there is more environmentally friendly stuff made of unbreakable glass, and you can go as far as buying the commercial kit, in standard sizes, made of stainless steel and in rectangular rather than round shapes so more can be stacked into a fridge.

A selection of small squeezy bottles is a good idea for liquids at the grill.

Standardize the types and sizes of container you use and don't let anyone else mess with them if they value their lives. There is nothing more guaranteed to mess up your workflow than missing or mismatched lids or your most vital container being pressed into service to take a particularly interesting beetle to school. I normally advocate a kind of easy-going Zen approach to kitchen work and sharing my workspace with family... but when it comes to Tupperware, I'm an extremist, absolutist zealot.

You will, of course, require cling film/plastic wrap, decent quality foil (don't buy a giant roll of the cheap stuff as I once did. I spent two years cursing and triple-wrapping chickens whose legs kept poking through the substandard and flimsy foil. My marriage only just survived). Big Green Egg supply a very good version of 'Peach Paper' the US butcher's paper that's become an essential for long, slow grill cooking. Have a roll of strong butcher's string. You can also beg from your butcher some heatproof rubber bands, which make trussing chickens much, much faster. You'll need a selection of skewers, large and small, metal and wooden. I also keep half a dozen stainless-steel roofing nails which work to transmit heat to the centre of dense food like whole potatoes or celeriac.

Paintbrushes are great for applying sauces and glazes. Go for 2-centimetre/1-inch width and pay enough so they don't shed hairs into your food.

THE LAST RULE

And one which is really so obvious, so deeply engrained in the mind of every serious cook and food lover that it shouldn't need saying...

Rule 4: Never, ever, ever wear a comedy apron.

PREP IS EVERYTHING

We love the image of the chef, clattering pans on the stove, shouting at the crew and firing great gouts of alcohol flame into the air. It makes great TV. It's also entirely unrepresentative of most of a professional cook's life because, in order to fling together great food in seconds 'on the line', someone (or more usually a whole crew of someones) has done a great deal of preparatory work. 'Prep' in cooking, as in so many other endeavours, is absolutely critical, but when home cooking outside, generally surrounded by friends, it's even more so.

The truth about outdoor cooking for many of us is that often it's not as much fun as we'd hoped. Things never go quite according to plan. Timings go awry, temperatures misbehave and soon you're struggling over hot food, swearing loudly and losing control. It's not good for the cook, it doesn't lead to great food and it's no fun for the guests. Prep prevents all of that, but it also has another secret advantage. When a chef walks out onto the line at the beginning of service, knowing that the prep is 'on point', they are relaxed and confident. That is precisely the feeling we want to have when we stand in front of the hot EGG – everything squared away, eventualities planned for and a game plan we can operate even when further relaxed by a couple of beers.

Recipes can go terribly wrong. I've lost track of the number of times they've gone wrong for me, and it's always for the same reason. I didn't read them all the way through first. These days I do it twice. Sure, it looks like a linear set of instructions that starts with a shopping list and ends with a picture of someone happily carrying a great groaning plate of food to happy people at a crowded table. However, for that result to occur, every step has to be followed, in order. If I get halfway through a recipe, reach out for the oregano and discover there isn't any, it's not because it's been stolen, it's evaporated or it's slipped through a wormhole in the space/time continuum, it's because I didn't notice it when I read the recipe (or didn't).

This effect is infinitely magnified if you're preparing a feast. More guests, more food, more courses.

Read each recipe through twice. Use the ingredients section to compile your shopping list and the 'method' steps to write your lists. Oh yes, I'm afraid there's writing too. You may have thought a chef's most important tool was a sharp knife. Nope. It's a Sharpie – one of those pens that writes anywhere, on anything, and the most frequently stolen piece of kit in a professional kitchen. There's even a special pocket for it in your white jacket.

You'll need four lists. (We've supplied some of these for you for these feasts, but when you go off-piste, you're on your own.)

1. SHOP LIST
Self-explanatory. Read through the ingredients section of each recipe you plan to use and compile the list to take with you to the butcher, fishmonger, grocery, deli, market or supermarket.

2. PREP LIST
A list of the things that can be peeled, cut, chopped, sliced, juiced, marinated, chilled, frozen or pre-cooked.

3. COOK LIST
The final steps you'll take, in the correct order, to transform the ingredients into the finished dishes at the right time.

4. FIRE LIST
The running order for the EGG. Remembering how easy it is to heat the EGG up and how much it's going to slow you down if you have to reduce the temperature, plan how you're going to manage the temperature over time, and list the equipment you're going to need to do this.

You might think you can keep all that stuff in your head and just wing it but, trust me, you can't. Even the most professional chef has a row of tickets in front of them to remind them what's next. I use a clipboard. You're probably going to need one too.

We've all got our tongs, spatulas, pokers and scrapers organized, but let's spare an early thought for plastic containers and Ziploc bags. Once you're standing by the EGG, there are only three things you should be doing: cooking, checking, or chatting wittily with your guests. All cutting and peeling should have been done well in advance, in the kitchen, with ingredients packed into containers, sealed and labelled. That's another reason for your marker pen. Before you drop your match into the charcoal you should have a pile of labelled containers that checks off against your list and gives you a feeling of total reassurance.

When you're cooking, the 'real estate' around the EGG is crowded and valuable, so try to keep your space entirely separate from your prep gear. If you're properly prepped, you shouldn't need a chopping board or a chef's knife anywhere near the EGG. They live in the kitchen. Carving knives and serving spoons should be on the table as only fully prepped components and ingredients and your personal mise-en-place deserve space out there. Anything else is a distraction or something that might go wrong.

Your mise-en-place should include pepper and salt, in whatever way you prefer them. You'll need lemons and possibly other citrus, cut and ready to squeeze. I like to keep some sherry vinegar, chilli (red pepper) flakes, olive oil and neutral oil to hand too. Depending on the cuisines you're working with, you might need soy, sesame oil, wine, mirin – anything you might need to squirt, spray or sprinkle while you cook. A set of squirt bottles will cost pence from a commercial kitchen supplier and you can also buy yourself a stainless-steel container to stand them all in. Your mise is yours alone. Like a Jedi light sabre, you need to plan it, build it, tweak it and protect it. The only rule is to keep it compact and efficient.

When you're planning, consider pre-cooking. If I'm doing a big feast, I often fire up the EGG the night before, pre-cook everything that will make my life easier, then pack, label and refrigerate. Lots of EGG dishes benefit from long, slow cooking and resting so, if I'm planning an afternoon or evening event, I often do some pre-cooking in the morning.

One final thought. Don't be a hero. Ask for help. Prep work is fun and congenial when shared. Appoint a child as runner and assistant when cooking (their little legs make them very good at running backwards and forwards to the kitchen). When the time comes to serve, consider getting the guests to do most of the work through a buffet or 'family-style' set up and, if you really do need to be formal, be sure to appoint someone competent as 'Front of House'.

BRUNCH

On weekend days when there's no rush for breakfast, the EGG is a brilliant way to cook things a little more substantial than the usual bacon and eggs. Particularly useful here is the recipe for proper baked beans. These can be prepared in a couple of hours but were traditionally prepared overnight in the dying heat of a campfire or bread oven. Follow the recipe for smoky beans or make some up when you're finishing an evening cook; close the dome and the vents and have the baked beans ready for brunch in the morning.

SERVES 8–12

FEAST MENU

SMOKY BEANS:
3–4 hours cooking time or overnight
140–170°C/275–325°F

CORN FRITTERS:
2 minutes for each fritter cooking
time 160–180°C/320–350°F

LOBSTER ROLLS:
3 minutes cooking time
160–180°C/320–350°F

**SALSICCE AND PEPPERS
WITH EGGS:**
Approx. 45 minutes cooking time
140–160°C/275–320°F

EGGS PIPERADE:
30 minutes cooking time
160–190°C/320–375°F

NOTE

Remember to burp your EGG when opening at high temperatures and cook with the dome closed.

EGG FEAST SET UP

(if cooking everything together as a feast)

Load and light your EGG. First of all your EGG target temp is 140–170°C/275–325°F; at this stage you will be cooking indirect. Add the convEGGtor with the legs up and the stainless steel grid sitting on top.

Next you will need to remove the previous set-up and cook direct. Add the convEGGtor basket with half moon plancha top left, stainless steel grid top right and a multi-level grid.

FEAST METHOD

(if cooking everything together as a feast)

1   Cook the smoky beans, set aside and keep warm until you are ready to serve.

2   Cook the corn fritters on the half moon plancha, set aside and keep warm.

3   Cook the lobster rolls, and eat instantly.

4   Start the salsicce and peppers in a skillet across the plancha and stainless steel grid, leave cooking the eggs until the last minute, move up to the multi-level grid (if you do not have this, keep the dish warm in an oven).

5   Start the eggs piperade in a paella pan across the plancha and stainless steel grid.

6   Finish by adding some oil onto the plancha and frying the eggs for the salsicce (placing on top of the sausages skillet when done), then crack eggs into the piperade and bake.

SMOKY BEANS

Serves 4

250g/1½ cups dried black beans (or use dried red kidney beans), soaked

2 onions,1 finely chopped, 1 cut in half

3 celery sticks, 2 finely chopped, 1 cut in half

4 garlic cloves, peeled and left whole

2 bay leaves

1–3 dried chipotle chillies (or use pasilla or ancho chillies), stems and seeds removed

1 tbsp red or white wine vinegar or cider vinegar

2 tsp honey, or soft brown sugar

2 tsp ground cumin

1 tsp Mexican dried oregano

1 green (bell) pepper, deseeded and finely chopped

3 tbsp lard, or neutral oil

2 tbsp tomato purée (paste)

Approx. 200g/7oz chopped leftover meat from a previous cook, or use diced smoked bacon, ham or chorizo (optional)

Salt and freshly ground black pepper (smoked salt can be good)

Feta, queso fresco or finely chopped coriander (cilantro), to serve (optional)

EGG SET UP
Indirect set-up; the convEGGtor in the legs-up position with the stainless steel grid on top of the convEGGtor legs.

TARGET TEMP
140–170°C/ 275–325°F

This is a kind of Mexican-inflected version of traditional Boston baked beans. They were originally cooked in a 'beanhole' – a hole dug in the ground in which a fire was lit before the beans were added in an earthenware pot and covered with soil. The beans cooked slowly overnight, a process that can easily be replicated in the EGG. And you can prepare the beans the day before. Remember to burp your EGG when opening at high temperatures.

Drain the soaked beans, rinse and add to a pot with enough fresh cold water to cover by 5cm/2in, bring to a boil on the hob and skim off any froth that appears. Add the halved onion, the celery halves, 1 garlic clove and the bay leaves and reduce the heat to low, place a lid on and cook for 1½–2 hours, or until the beans are tender. If the beans get too dry, top up with more water. When tender, drain and reserve the liquid for adding to the beans later on.

Open the preheated EGG and dry-fry the dried chillies and the remaining 3 garlic cloves in a preheated skillet or cast-iron Dutch oven for a minute or so with the dome closed, turning often until aromatic. Open the dome and add just enough boiling water to cover, leave on the heat and cook for a few minutes with the dome closed. Remove the pan and drain, saving the liquid, and then blend using a pestle and mortar to a coarse paste using a little of the reserved liquid if needed. Add the vinegar, honey or sugar, cumin and oregano.

Open the EGG and, with the same pan, fry the chopped onions, celery and green pepper in the lard for 10 minutes with the dome closed until soft, then open, add the chipotle paste and tomato purée and cook for a minute or so until rich and thick.

Open the dome and add the drained beans, including the bay leaves, and enough of the reserved liquid to cover, then stir in the meat (if using).

Put the lid on the pan, close the dome and cook for 1½–2 hours (or leave in the cooling EGG overnight) until the beans are tender. If the beans get too dry, top up with more stock or water. Throw away the bay leaves and season to taste. Serve topped with feta, queso fresco or chopped coriander, if you like.

CORN FRITTERS

Serves 2–4

200g/7oz fresh sweetcorn
(corn) kernels

3 eggs

100ml/scant ½ cup buttermilk, or
use thinned natural (plain) yoghurt
(thin it with a little cold water)

100g/¾ cup self-raising
(self-rising) flour

50g/⅓ cup fine cornmeal, or polenta

50g/1¾oz Cheddar cheese or similar,
coarsely grated or crumbled

2 tbsp finely chopped parsley or
chives

½ tsp sugar

Vegetable or olive oil, for frying

Salt and freshly ground black pepper

Drizzle of honey, to serve

Corn fritters are usually deep-fried – and very good they are too – but I reckon they taste better when treated like little thick pancakes and cooked on the plancha. Keep the temperature low and keep the fritters moving on the hot metal so they cook through without scorching too far on the outside.

In a blender, blend the sweetcorn kernels with the eggs and buttermilk until very smooth.

Put the flour and cornmeal or polenta in a bowl and whisk in the egg mixture. Stir in the cheese and herbs. Season with the sugar, a pinch of salt and a little black pepper.

Burp your preheated EGG, open the dome and heat a film of oil on the plancha or in a skillet, then add several heaped tablespoonfuls of the batter (you'll need to cook these in small batches) and cook for 1 minute or until the bottoms have firmed enough to flip over, then flip and fry on the other side for another 1 minute. When cooked, transfer to a warm serving plate and cover with a clean dish towel.

Continue frying the remaining pancakes/fritters in the same way in small batches until all the batter is used up. Remember to cook with the dome closed.

Serve warm, drizzled with honey.

EGG SET UP
Direct set-up; the stainless steel grid with the plancha or a skillet on top.

TARGET TEMP
160–180°C/320–350°F

LOBSTER ROLLS

Lobster rolls are a favourite treat in the North-eastern United States, and they're usually made with steamed lobsters with either a delicate dressing of mayo and celery or a little melted butter. I think they taste infinitely better if the lobster is grilled in the shell for maximum flavour and you serve them with butter and mayonnaise.

Serves 2–4

2 whole raw lobsters, halved lengthways, intestinal tract removed

100g/7 tbsp salted butter

2 garlic cloves, finely chopped

1–2 tsp chilli flakes (red pepper flakes), or cayenne pepper

1 sprig of thyme

1 tsp black peppercorns

1 pared strip of lemon or orange zest

Juice of ½ lemon

Salt and freshly ground black pepper

To serve

Handful of mixed chopped herbs, such as chives, parsley, tarragon and chervil

80g/2¾oz mayonnaise

Bread rolls, split in half

Finely chopped gherkins or capers (optional)

Remove the lobster legs and crack them with the back of a knife. Pile them all into the butter in a large pan and simmer over a low heat to extract the flavour. Strain the butter and throw away the legs.

Simmer the garlic, chilli flakes or cayenne pepper, thyme, peppercorns and citrus zest in the same butter (in the same pan) for about 30 seconds, then take off the heat and leave to infuse.

EGG SET UP
Direct set-up with the stainless steel grill or cast-iron grill, with the plancha for the latter part of the method.

TARGET TEMP
160–180°C/320–350°F

Mix the chopped herbs into the mayonnaise in a small bowl, ready to serve. Set aside.

Gently crack the lobster claws. Burp the preheated EGG and place the lobster halves, flesh-side down, on the grill, for 1 minute, then flip and spoon 1 tablespoon of the flavoured butter over the flesh.

Cook for another 1–2 minutes with the dome closed until the meat is just cooked and pulls away from the shell.

Transfer to a tray and leave until cool enough to handle, pouring over any remaining flavoured butter and adding the lemon juice.

Remove the flesh from the lobster tails and place in a bowl. Pull the claws apart, remove that flesh and add to the bowl. If you like, remove the tomalley and roe and chop. Cut the flesh into nice-sized pieces, then pour over the buttery juices and season to taste with salt and pepper.

To serve, spread the cut sides of the rolls with the herby mayonnaise, then place them face-down on the plancha. They will fry in the oil from the mayo, leaving a crisp, delicately golden eggy crust.

Fill the rolls with the lobster meat and juices and top with chopped gherkins or capers, if you like.

SALSICCE AND PEPPERS WITH EGGS

Sausages and peppers is an old diner favourite. One of those dishes that defines Italian American eating but may be too everyday and domestic to be claimed by any region in The Old Country. It requires the kind of long 'stewing' at which the EGG excels and also, though this is not part of any original recipe, benefits from a touch of smoke. Above all, it's made mind-blowing by the very diner-ish addition of a runny fried egg. These quantities are to serve two but can be sized up. 12 sausages and 4 or 6 eggs look unbelievably cool in a Big Green Egg paella pan or similar. And yes, I know the number of (bell) peppers looks but, trust me, it's the way they lose their water content and stew down in their own juice that really makes this so much more than a quick snack at the counter.

Serves 6

6 Italian salsicce (sausages), fennel-flavoured
Boiling water, to cover
About 75ml/2½fl oz olive oil
2 red (bell) peppers
1 green (bell) pepper
2 yellow (bell) peppers
1 sweet Ramiro pepper (optional)
1 small hot red chilli (dried is fine)
1 onion
4 garlic cloves, crushed
2 eggs
Salt and freshly ground black pepper

Using the direct set-up, add the sausages to a skillet, add enough boiling water to come halfway up their sides, then poach in the simmering water. You can start this early, while the EGG is still coming up to temperature. Once the internal temperature of the sausages reaches 65°C/149°F, remove them and put on a plate. Save the poaching water in a jug and let the sausages sit around to consider their life choices. If you want to prep ahead, this can be done a day before and the sausages kept in the fridge. Pre-poaching is a good restaurant trick for making sure sausages are cooked properly through, but it can allow some of the flavour out and into the water which is then poured away... which would be a waste... which is why we're definitely not doing that.

Increase the EGG's temperature to 180°C/350°F by opening the draft door and rEGGulator in slight increments until that temperature is sustained.

Pour a hefty glug of olive oil into the same skillet, roll the sausages in it, burp and open the preheated EGG and put the skillet on the grill, then close the dome and allow the sausages to brown while you deseed all the peppers and the chilli, peel the onion and chop them all into coarse chunks.

Burp and open the EGG, lifting the sausages out of the oil and put them aside, then stir all the chopped peppers, chilli and onion and the crushed garlic into the residual oil. Stir things up a bit, then pour the sausage poaching water over, close the

continued overleaf...

EGG SET UP
Direct set-up; the stainless steel grid with a skillet on top.

TARGET TEMP
160–180°C/320–350°F

dome and close the vents a little (you can throw a small handful of smoking chips into the EGG at this stage, if you wish).

The veg will now be steaming, getting a little smoky and the temperature will be dropping. Burp and check occasionally and, once almost all the water has boiled off, season with salt and pepper, add a glug more oil if you think it needs it, and stir everything around. Now bury the sausages in the pepper mixture, top the skillet with a lid or foil and put it back in the EGG and close the dome. Rest and drink beer.

The point now is to keep things slow until the peppers achieve the right texture. Peeled peppers are, for some reason, completely rubbish in this dish. They need the skins to hold things together, but they need long cooking so the skins become velvety, no less than 30 minutes. Don't omit the green pepper either, even if you can't stand the things. It adds a lovely vegetal edge and stops things getting too sweet.

As soon as the peppers are irresistible, you are pretty much done. Open the dome, taste, adjust the seasoning, then spoon the vegetables onto two plates and distribute the sausages between them, arranging them artfully on top. Pour over all the remaining juices, then quickly wipe the skillet with paper towels, pour a splash more olive oil in, open the vents, open the dome and fry the two eggs till the whites are set but the yolks are still runny. Serve on top of the sausages and peppers.

EGGS PIPERADE

Eggs piperade is a traditional Basque dish, making full use of the plentiful local capsicums, which are stewed – as in the sausage dish previously – but with the addition of espelette pepper, a local aromatic hot chilli that's dried and ground. You can, if you wish, substitute Turkish, Italian or Korean chilli/pepper flakes, each of which bring their own unique fragrance. Eggs are then baked in the stewed pepper sauce, shakshuka-style, and topped with melted broken lumps of cheese. Burp your EGG when opening at high temperatures and keep the dome closed when cooking.

Serves 6

1 onion, finely diced

2 red (bell) peppers, deseeded and finely diced

1 green (bell) pepper, deseeded and finely diced

3 tbsp olive oil

3 garlic cloves, finely chopped

5g ground espelette pepper

10g/¼oz flat-leaf parsley, finely chopped

3 large tomatoes, skinned, deseeded and chopped

½ tsp salt, plus an extra pinch

50g/1¾oz soft goat's cheese, cut into 2cm/¾in cubes

6 eggs

Open the preheated EGG and in a wide, skillet or Big Green Egg paella pan, gently fry the onion and red and green peppers in the olive oil for 10–15 minutes with until very soft, stirring often.

Open the dome, add the garlic, half the espelette pepper and half the parsley and cook for about 2 minutes, then add the tomatoes and salt and cook, uncovered, with the dome closed, for a further 5 or so minutes until the tomatoes are thick and rich.

Open the EGG, dot over the goat's cheese, then use a spoon to make six holes in the sauce, crack an egg into each and sprinkle over the remaining espelette pepper and a further pinch of salt. Close the EGG and cook for 4–6 minutes, or until the eggs are cooked to the desired consistency.

Serve topped with the remaining parsley.

EGG SET UP
Indirect set-up; the convEGGtor in the legs-up position with the stainless steel grid on top of the convEGGtor legs.

TARGET TEMP
160–190°C/320–375°F

SPANISH-STYLE FEAST

Spanish cooking has taken the world by storm in recent years, and for good reason. Their ingredients are of superb quality, they seem to excel at every level of cooking from street food to the very hautest of cuisine, and their range of techniques runs the gamut from live fire, through clay ovens, specialist pots, griddles and planchas to the madness of the molecular. The EGG, then, versatile as it is, is the ideal tool for experimenting with Spanish cooking. In this case, there's so much to choose from, the only difficulty is to reduce it to a single feast.

Big Green Egg supply a plancha, the commonest grill in Spanish cookery, and a range of excellent paella pans – which we use here to assemble the centrepiece. Nothing says 'feast' quite as well as a single large dish, hot from the fire and carried in by two people.

There are plenty of interesting techniques here but I'm quietly fascinated by tombet, a sort of Mallorquin ratatouille that seems to go well with all sorts of dishes from other traditions and, while prepping a whole octopus from scratch might seem a stretch for some cooks, the poaching liquid created as a by-product is one of the most life-altering stocks you'll ever produce. There are two other flavour notes key to Spanish cookery: saffron and pimentón or smoked paprika. Both of these are now widely available but it's best not to skimp. The best fresh stuff can be expensive but it's worth every penny.

SERVES 8–10

FEAST MENU
EGGLESS ALIOLI

TOMBET:
1 hour cooking time
150–180°C/300–350°F

FIDEUÀ:
30 minutes cooking time
170–190°C/325–375°F

CARABIÑEROS PRAWNS:
5 minutes cooking time
180–200°C/350–400°F

GRILLED OCTOPUS:
5 minutes cooking time
180–200°C/350–400°F

EGG FEAST SET UP
(if cooking everything together as
a feast)

Load and light your EGG. Bring
it to 150C/300°F and add the
convEGGtor basket with the half
moon cast-iron searing grid top
right (direct side), half moon baking
stone bottom left and stainless steel
grid top left (indirect side). When
needed, increase your EGG
temperature to 180°C/350°F.

FEAST METHOD
(if cooking everything together as a feast)

1   Cook the raw octopus in the kitchen (if
buying raw).

2   Make the tombet at 150°C/300°F, grill the
veg on the direct side and start the sauce
on the indirect side. Off the heat, place the
veg and sauce in layers, then the potatoes
and herbs and finish cooking on the baking
stone side.

3   Make the alioli while the tombet is cooking.

4   Add the multi-level grid. Bring the
temperature up to 180°C/350°F and
cook the fideuà whilst reheating the
tombet above on the top level of the
EGGspander system.

5   Grill the octopus and prawns on the
bottom grid, adding some to the fideuà
to finish.

NOTES

1   Have all your ingredients ready to go for
all the recipes before you start to cook
the tombet.

2   If you've cooked fresh octopus, use the
octopus cooking liquid as the base for the
stock (topping it up with water). You could
also use the prawn (shrimp) heads to make
stock if you're not going to eat them.
Octopus is also available cooked.

3   You could use a shallow cast-iron pan for
the fideuà if you don't have a paella pan.

4   You could use paella rice instead of
vermicelli – increase the cooking time to
20–25 minutes.

5   Remember to burp your EGG when opening
at high temperatures and cook with the
dome closed.

6   There is plenty of flavour in the juices in
the grilled prawn heads, but if you're a bit
squeamish about crunching straight in,
you can squeeze them over the fideuà.

7   Grill the octopus side-by-side with the
prawns if you've got space. If not, cook
the octopus first.

8   Serve with lemon wedges, finger bowls
and napkins.

EGGLESS ALIOLI

There is no end to the versatility of mayonnaises when it comes to outdoor cooking. Most of them, including the massively garlicky aïoli from southern France, use egg yolk to help the oil emulsify, but this version, from just over the border in Cataluña, is the macho real-deal. A true Catalan makes alioli by smushing garlic to a paste with the side of a knife and then using it to emulsify the oil. There's no other ingredient apart from a little salt and pepper. It's best made in a pestle and mortar and can be done in a food processor, but for real authenticity, you can whip it up with the flat of the knife blade on a flat plate. This takes self-confidence bordering on the arrogant, but it can be done.

Note: Keep an egg about you. If you find your alioli is splitting, repeat the method, whisking or blending the split mix into an egg yolk, and call it aïoli. Make this while the tombet cooks.

Blend together the garlic, a pinch of salt, a little black pepper and 2 tablespoons of water in a pestle and mortar or a food processor for 30–60 seconds until you have a paste.

Add 1 teaspoon of the olive oil in a thin drizzle while mixing, then another and another. Then add the remaining oil in a thin stream while mixing to a nice thick consistency. Adjust the seasoning to taste with salt and pepper.

Makes 300ml/1¼ cups

1 head of garlic, peeled and thinly sliced
Salt and freshly ground black pepper
250ml/generous 1 cup olive oil

TOMBET

Serves 4

2 large aubergines (eggplants), sliced lengthways into 1cm/½in-thick slices, lightly salted and left to drain for 10 minutes in a colander, then patted dry

8 tbsp olive oil

4 courgettes (zucchini), sliced lengthways into 1cm/½in-thick slices

2 small onions, thinly sliced

2 big garlic cloves, finely sliced

Pinch of pimentón/smoked paprika

400g/14oz tomato passata (puréed tomatoes)

2 tsp dried oregano

500g/1lb 2oz waxy potatoes, boiled until just tender, drained, cooled and thinly sliced

Small bunch of flat-leaf parsley, roughly chopped

Salt and freshly ground black pepper

EGG SET UP
Direct set-up with the stainless steel grid or cast-iron grid.

Then...
Indirect set-up; the convEGGtor in the legs-up position with the stainless steel grid or cast-iron grid on top of the convEGGtor legs.

TARGET TEMP
150–180°C/300–350°F

Tombet, or more accurately *tumbet Mallorquin*, is a simple preparation of local vegetables from the Balearic islands. In Mallorca the veg would be individually fried in olive oil before stacking and finishing them in the oven - much like a good ratatouille. In this recipe, though, we've grilled the oiled veg and then added the moisture with a tomato base. It ends up just as juicy and filling and, with the tomato flavour properly distributed through, it becomes not just an excellent side but also works as a vegetarian main on its own. Remember to burp your EGG when opening at high temperatures.

Once the EGG is up to temperature, brush the aubergine slices with 2 tablespoons of the olive oil, open the dome and grill for 4–6 minutes on each side. Turn regularly until soft and golden brown all over.

Brush the courgette slices with 2 more tablespoons of olive oil, and with the dome open, grill for 3–5 minutes on each side, until tender and beginning to brown. Take out the aubergine and courgette slices.

Add the sliced onions, garlic and 2 tablespoons of olive oil in a heated pan or skillet and fry for 10 minutes with the dome closed until soft. Add the pimentón and stir through. Open the dome to add the tomato passata and half the oregano and cook for 10 minutes, then stir, season with salt and pepper and remove from the heat.

Remove the grid and add the convEGGtor into an indirect position, with the legs facing up and the stainless steel grid sitting on top, close the dome and regulate the temperature until the EGG reaches 180°C/350°F.

Arrange a third of the aubergine slices in the base of a cast-iron dish, then top with a third each of the courgette slices and the tomato sauce. Repeat these layers, finishing off with a layer of potato slices. Drizzle with a little more oil.

Scatter with the remaining dried oregano and spoon over a final tablespoon of olive oil.

Roast for 25–35 minutes, with the dome closed, until the top is golden and has crisped up. Remove and put to one side to serve at room temperature, while you cook the fideuà. Serve sprinkled with the parsley.

Note: You can add (deseeded) red or green (bell) peppers if you want, either to the sauce or grill them.

FIDEUÀ

Serves 4

80ml/⅓ cup extra-virgin olive oil

2 onions, finely chopped

2 red (bell) peppers or 1 red and 1 green (bell) pepper, deseeded and finely chopped

6 garlic cloves, finely chopped

2 tsp sweet paprika

1 x 400g/14oz can chopped plum tomatoes

Big pinch of saffron strands, soaked in a little warm water for about 10 minutes

1.2L/5 cups fish stock (or water)

600g/1lb 5oz dried vermicelli pasta

800g/1lb 12oz mixed raw whole prawns (shrimp), white fish (cut into small chunks) and prepped squid flesh

Salt and freshly ground black pepper

A fideuà has a lot in common with a paella but uses pasta instead of rice. It's a special, thin vermicelli that's cut into short lengths. The thing that makes fideuà just a little bit more interesting than paella, is the way that some of the short pasta pieces stick up out of the liquid as the dish cooks and actually wave around. These bits will crisp up, creating an entirely unusual texture and flavour combination. There is nothing better than the EGG for cooking fideuà, as the closed dome forms a perfect replica of the charcoal-fuelled clay oven in which it would traditionally have been cooked. Remember to burp your EGG when opening at high temperatures.

Once the EGG has reached 190°C/375°F, add the paella pan to preheat.

Add the olive oil, then the onions, peppers and garlic to the pan and cook to soften for at least 10 minutes with the dome closed.

Open the EGG and add the paprika, tomatoes and saffron with its soaking water. Let the mixture cook for about 5 minutes, then add the preheated stock (or water) and bring to a simmer. Add a generous amount of salt.

Add the vermicelli to the pan in a very even layer, carefully shaking the pan gently as you do, so that the mixture evens out. After a few minutes, as the pasta begins to soften, place the prawns, fish and squid carefully on top. They will cook in the flavoured steam and drip any spare juices back into the pan.

Close the dome and cook for about 10–15 minutes, then remove from the heat and rest for at least 10 minutes.

Serve straight from the pan, scraping up any baked-on bits from the bottom (these are the best), with the alioli on the side to stir in.

EGG SET UP
Direct set-up with the stainless steel grid or cast-iron grid, with a paella pan sitting on top.

TARGET TEMP
170–190°C/
325–375°F

CARABIÑEROS PRAWNS

1 large or 2–3 small–medium
Carabiñeros prawns (shrimp)
per person, whole (or use other
sustainably-caught whole
wild prawns)

Olive oil

Flaky sea salt

½ lemon, cut into wedges,
to serve

Carabiñeros are Spanish prawns (shrimp) with a deep red colour. They're named after the border and shore patrol regiments and the fetching colour of their uniform lapels. They are also huge, the size of a junior lobster or a langoustine that's spent too much time at the gym. They are quite difficult to find so do substitute with the largest fresh prawns you can find. The key thing with this dish, though, is not to waste all the gloopy, juicy loveliness in the heads. If you can't quite bring yourself to suck it, be sure to squeeze it out and stir it into your fideuà.

Toss the prawns with some oil and flaky salt.

Burp and open your preheated EGG and grill the prawns with the dome closed for about 1½–2½ minutes on each side (depending on size) or until the shells are just beginning to toast and char, and the flesh is just cooked through.

Serve on top of the fideuà with the lemon wedges, adding any juices.

EGG SET UP
Direct set-up with
the plancha or
stainless steel grid
in place. Ensure you
preheat the plancha
or grid.

TARGET TEMP
180–200°C/350–400°F

GRILLED OCTOPUS

1 cooked octopus tentacle per person
Olive oil, for dressing
1 garlic clove, very finely chopped
20g/¾oz parsley, finely chopped
Dusting of smoked paprika
½ lemon, cut into wedges, to serve

Octopus used to be a rarity in fishmongers. They were considered difficult to prepare and they rather freaked out a lot of home cooks. Today they are plentiful and easy to get hold of pre-cooked. Fishermen prepare them in individual single-tentacle servings, which are sealed into plastic pouches and cooked 'sous-vide'. This ensures no flavour is lost and gives an incredible shelf-life to a delicious and nourishing ingredient. If you do cook your own octopus, the braising liquid is the most incredible stock, and is particularly good for slow-braising pork shoulder. Don't knock it 'til you've tried it.

Burp and open your preheated EGG, then grill the octopus tentacles for about 2 minutes on each side, with the dome closed, until heated through. You are looking for even char and caramelization.

Slice the tentacles and dress with some olive oil, the garlic, parsley and a dusting of paprika. Serve on top of the fideuà with the lemon wedges, adding any juices.

EGG SET UP
Direct set-up with the plancha or stainless steel grid in place. Make sure your cooking surface is preheated.

TARGET TEMP
180–200°C/350–400°F

PIZZA PARTY

Pizza was invented in Naples and they take it pretty seriously there. There's a society that makes, transmits and enforces the rules about True Pizza. Apparently, there are only two types: 'Marinara' (tomato, oil, oregano and garlic) and 'Margherita' (tomato, oil, mozzarella or fior di latte, grated cheese and basil). There are dozens of specifications about flour, dough and rising times and very particular instructions on cooking, and here, I quote: 'Cooking surface temperature: 380–430°C. Oven dome temperature: 485°C. Cooking time: about 60–90 seconds'.

It's pretty incredible. The full instructions are freely available online if you want to get authentic. Can you achieve that kind of cooking environment in your kitchen? Not a chance. Can you do it in your EGG? It's really quite possible.

This feast, though, is based on some less obsessive pizza cooking techniques at slightly less terrifying temperatures. In a pizzeria, one person, the pizzaiolo, does the cooking and assistants set up the pizzas. Cooking pizzas in the EGG requires similar focus and concentration, so it can be fun to have your guests or kids setting the pizzas up while you work the 'oven'.

SERVES 6–8

FEAST MENU
SOURDOUGH PIZZA BASE

CONVENTIONAL PIZZA DOUGH VARIATION: 4–8 minutes cooking time 300°C/570°F

- - MARGHERITA
- - GARLIC AND HERB
- - POTATO AND ROSEMARY

FOCACCIA PIZZA: 30 minutes cooking time 220–240°C/425–475°F

PEACH SALAD: 5 minutes cooking 180–200°C/350–400°F

FEAST METHOD
(if cooking everything together as a feast)

1   Prepare the dough in advance.

2   Prepare all of the pizza toppings.

3   Cook the foccacia.

4   Cook the peach salad.

5   Build and cook the pizzas.

EGG FEAST SET UP
(if cooking everything together as a feast)

Load and light your EGG. Firstly, bring your EGG to the target temperature of 200–220°C/ 400–425°F; you will be cooking indirect. Set up your convEGGtor with the legs facing down onto the fire ring, place the stainless steel grid on top, then your baking stone on top of that. This will be to cook the focaccia pizza.

Secondly, keeping the EGG set-up the same, increase the temperature to 300°C/570°F. You will know when your baking stone is hot enough to cook on when a healthy sprinkling of flour turns a golden brown in 4-5 minutes. When cooking pizzas, make sure you give your EGG ample time to heat up the ceramics evenly; this is easily achievable with a full load of charcoal.

NOTES

1   Have all of your toppings, tomato sauce, flour and dough balls ready in separate bowls and containers.

2   When loading and lighting the EGG, you must be generous with the charcoal, this is not the time to be frugal. You will need a healthy amount of charcoal to reach and sustain the high temperatures needed to cook pizzas.

3   Light your EGG in advance of when you want to serve your pizza. You need to make sure the baking stone and the EGG ceramics have been preheated well.

4   Have your cooking equipment set up and to hand: wooden pizza peel for building the pizza on and putting it onto the baking stone, a metal peel for turning and removing the pizza from the baking stone and a metal brush or spatula to clean the stone in between pizzas.

5   To test whether your baking stone is hot and ready to cook on, sprinkle some flour on the stone and close the EGG. When the flour has cooked and turned brown, the stone is ready to cook on. Be careful not to let the flour burn and clean off before adding your first pizza.

6   You are cooking at extremely high temperatures, make sure you cautiously burp your EGG when opening, and cook with the dome closed.

SOURDOUGH PIZZA BASE

Nothing beats a good sourdough base on a pizza, not just for the exceptional taste, but also the gluten strength of long, slow risen dough makes it easier to stretch it thin for a gloriously crispy finish. Some Italian delis sell flour specifically for pizza bases with added durum wheat, which pumps up the gluten even further. In the unlikely event you have any dough left over, keep it in the fridge overnight. It makes amazing flatbreads a day later.

You probably need to start this first thing in the morning for baking in the evening, or even the night before, and your starter needs to be active.

Mix everything, apart from the salt, together in a large mixing bowl until all the liquid is absorbed into a rough dough.

Cover with a damp dish towel for 20 minutes for the flour to completely hydrate, then use wet hands to fold in the salt.

Cover with a damp dish towel and leave to ferment for anything from 3–8 hours (or even longer depending on temperature/starter condition) until the dough has nearly doubled in sixe. For the first 3–4 hours, every 45 minutes or so, use wet hands to lift, stretch and fold the dough to strengthen it.

Scrape the dough onto a floured surface and use flour to cut it into four even pieces. Fold each round of dough in on itself, to give a round shape. Cover and leave to prove for a couple of hours.

Makes 4 large pizzas

400g/3 cups strong white bread flour or special pizza base flour, plus extra for dusting

250ml/9fl oz tepid water

150g/5½oz active sourdough starter

1 tsp salt

CONVENTIONAL PIZZA DOUGH VARIATION

Put the yeast into a big mixing bowl and mix in the tepid water with a spoon. Leave it to bubble for 5 minutes, and then add the flour and salt and mix well to combine completely into a dough.

Place a damp dish towel over the bowl and leave for 5 minutes. Oil your hands, then remove the dough from the bowl and knead it on an oiled surface for 5 minutes until supple and smooth.

Cover and leave to rise until almost doubled in size, about 1–1½ hours.

When you are nearly ready to cook the pizzas, divide the dough into four even pieces and roll into balls, then cover and leave to prove for an hour or so to allow air pockets to form.

Makes 4 large pizzas

1 tsp dried active yeast granules

340ml/scant 1½ cups tepid water

450g/3¼ cups strong white bread flour or '00' flour

1 tsp salt

Olive oil, for oiling your hands and surface for initial kneading, and for drizzling to serve

EGG SET UP

Make the dough before lighting the EGG.

Direct set-up with the convEGGtor legs down and a baking stone on top of the stainless steel grid. Ensure to preheat the pizza stone.

TARGET TEMP
300°C/570°F

TO SHAPE THE PIZZA DOUGH

Have a pizza peel or thin boards ready and dust them lightly with flour or a flour semolina mix.

Delicately stretch each portion of dough into a 25–30cm/ 10–12in round, trying as best you can to preserve the air pockets. Move one onto the peel by sliding the peel underneath, then add your topping; be careful not to overload your pizza with toppings as it will not cook evenly, the base will cook quicker than the toppings. It can be worth gently sliding the pizza back and forth on the peel to make sure it doesn't stick.

Burp your EGG and slowly open. Slide the pizza onto the hot baking stone and cook for 4–8 minutes with the dome closed. This really does depend on temperature – as you open and close the EGG, the temperature can rise quite quickly. You may also find hot spots on your baking stone so if you feel the need to turn the pizzas for a more even cook, do so. When operating the EGG at these temperatures, please make sure you burp the EGG and open the dome slowly.

Slide the cooked pizza onto a large plate or a board and drizzle with a bit more olive oil, then season with some salt and pepper, if you like. Serve.

Repeat with the remaining pizza dough portions and topping.

PIZZA TOPPINGS

All toppings are enough for 4 pizzas

'MARGHERITA'

1 x 400g/14oz can chopped tomatoes,
drained and crushed

1 big bunch of basil, leaves torn,
plus extra to serve

200g/7oz mozzarella, drained and
cut into small pieces

Salt and freshly ground black pepper

Infuse the crushed tomatoes with the basil
and season to taste with salt and pepper.

Spread the tomato sauce over the pizza bases
and top with the mozzarella. Cook one pizza
at a time in the preheated EGG, for 4–8 minutes,
depending on the temperature of the EGG.
Once cooked, garnish with the extra basil leaves
and serve.

GARLIC AND HERB

150g/⅔ cup butter, softened

2 garlic cloves, crushed

3 tbsp finely chopped parsley

Salt and freshly ground black pepper

Mix all of the ingredients together in a bowl,
seasoning with salt and pepper, then keep
somewhere where it will stay soft and
spreadable.

Spread a quarter of the flavoured butter over
each pizza base, then cook one pizza at a time in
the preheated EGG for 4–8 minutes.

POTATO AND ROSEMARY

300g/10½oz new potatoes, scrubbed and
very thinly sliced (you could use a mandoline)

2 sprigs of rosemary, leaves picked
and finely chopped

2 garlic cloves, finely chopped

½ small red onion, very thinly sliced

2 tbsp extra-virgin olive oil

Grated fresh Parmesan cheese

Handful of rocket (arugula) leaves

Salt and freshly ground black pepper

Mix the potatoes, rosemary, garlic and onion together with the
olive oil in a bowl and season with salt and pepper.

Distribute the potato mixture thinly over the pizza bases,
then cook one pizza at a time on the preheated EGG for
4–8 minutes. Top with Parmesan and rocket before serving.

FOCACCIA PIZZA

Serves 4

400ml/1¾ cups tepid water

10g/¼oz dried active yeast granules

500g/3⅔ cups strong white
bread flour

½ tsp flaky sea salt

6 tbsp extra-virgin olive oil

1 sprig of rosemary, leaves picked
and finely chopped

2 garlic cloves, thinly sliced

200g/7oz canned chopped tomatoes,
or use chopped peeled fresh tomatoes

1 small bunch of basil

100g/3½oz mozzarella, drained and
coarsely grated

100g/3½oz Cheddar cheese,
coarsely grated

Salt and freshly ground black pepper

This is sometimes referred to as 'Detroit' pizza and it was supposedly originally made in the kind of iron tray they use in a garage under a car engine to catch oil leaks. Square-sided and 5cm/2in or so deep, it uses focaccia dough, which rises high and airy and requires a sprinkling of cheap Cheddar around the edges before cooking. This renders into a kind of cheesy oil that seeps down the sides of the pizza and fries the edges of the base. God it's good.

Stir together the tepid water and yeast in a large mixing bowl and leave it to sit for 5 minutes until frothy.

Add the flour, salt and 2 tablespoons of the olive oil to the yeast mixture and mix well, either by hand or using the dough hook on a stand mixer, for about 10 minutes until it becomes a bit less sticky, adding the rosemary towards the end.

Tip into a clean large bowl brushed with olive oil, then cover with a clean dish towel and leave it to rise in a warm place for about 1–1½ hours until it has doubled in size.

Brush a large, deep baking tray, 25 x 20 x 5.5cm (10 x 8 x 2¼in) with olive oil. Tip the dough onto the tray and use your fingertips to flatten the dough, then brush the top with more olive oil. Cover and leave for 20 minutes.

Dip your fingers in olive oil and press and stretch the dough into the edges of the baking tray, leaving the dimples from your fingers. Cover again with the dish towel and leave it to prove in a warm place for about 40 minutes.

Meanwhile, cook the garlic in a little olive oil in a pan for 1–2 minutes until fragrant, then add the tomatoes and basil and cook for 5 minutes until rich and thick. Season with salt and pepper.

Spoon the tomato mixture on top of the focaccia dough, quite unevenly, using the spoon to push it into the dimples here and there. Sprinkle the mozzarella over the top and drizzle with olive oil.

Sprinkle the Cheddar all around the border of the pizza, then use a palette knife to separate the pizza a little from the baking tray, allowing the oil and cheese to slip down the edges.

Burp and open the preheated EGG and bake the pizza for 25 minutes, cooking with the dome closed until the top is nicely coloured and the base is crisp, drizzling with the remaining tablespoon or so of oil as it comes out. Cut into squares before serving.

EGG SET UP
Indirect set-up; the convEGGtor in the legs-up position with the stainless steel grid on top of the legs. Or set up your convEGGtor with the legs facing down onto the fire ring, place the stainless steel grid on top, and your baking stone on top of that.

TARGET TEMP
220–240°C/425–475°F

PEACH AND TOMATO SALAD

Serves 2–4

4 tbsp extra-virgin olive oil

3 tbsp red or white wine vinegar or cider vinegar

½ small red onion, very thinly sliced

1 tbsp sugar

2 ripe peaches, stoned (pitted) and halved

400g/14oz tomatoes, cut into thin wedges

Small bunch of basil, leaves picked

Salt and freshly ground black pepper

If you can find a superbly ripe juicy peach for this salad, you're welcome to use it, but I urge you instead to eat it by itself. Really gloriously juicy peaches seem to be getting rarer, but this recipe uses the searing power of the EGG to slightly caramelise the peach and get the juices to run. It actually works better with the slightly less sumptuous peaches we've grown used to in the supermarket. This is a devastating combination with the tartness of little tomatoes.

Mix the oil and 2 tablespoons of the vinegar together in a bowl and stir in the red onion, then add salt and pepper to taste and put to one side to macerate.

Mix together the sugar and remaining tablespoon of vinegar on a large plate, then press the cut side of each peach into the sugar mixture to coat. Burp and open your preheated EGG, heat a large skillet and add the peaches, cut-side down, and cook until the sugar and juices caramelize, for about 3-4 minutes with the dome closed. As the peaches caramelize, turn them over and cook for 1–2 minutes until tender. Allow to cool, then thinly slice.

About 10 minutes before serving, gently toss the peaches, tomatoes and half the basil with the onion mixture and season lightly with a little more salt and pepper. Set aside for the 10 minutes to allow the flavours to infuse a little.

Scatter with the remaining basil to serve.

EGG SET UP
Direct set-up with the stainless steel grid or cast-iron grid.

TARGET TEMP
180–200°C/350–400°F

CURRY NIGHT

If, like me, you're a fan of South Asian food, the EGG is an excellent companion. The EGG/wok combination can operate in a very similar way to the karahi, the cooking/frying pot common across the subcontinent. Skewers of meat can be hung through the vent hole at the top of the EGG to create a passable replica of a tandoor and it's even possible to slap naan on the inside of the dome for authentic scorching. This feast makes no claims to authenticity though and is based on the simple and popular chicken bhuna.

SERVES 6–8

FEAST MENU
CHICKEN CURRY:
1½ hours cooking time
180°C/350°F

BAKED PILAU:
1 hour cooking time
160–180°C/320–350°F

RAITA

STUFFED GREEN CHILLIES:
4 minutes cooking time
180°C/350°F

BRINGJAL PICKLE:
40–45 minutes cooking time
180°C/350°F

EGG FEAST SET UP
(if cooking everything together as a feast)

Load and light your EGG. Bring it to 180°C/350°F and add the convEGGtor basket with half moon cast-iron searing grid top right, half moon baking stone bottom left, stainless steel grid top left and, later, a multi-level grid.

FEAST METHOD
(if cooking everything together as a feast)

1   Make the Aubergine pickle; either cook this dirty on the charcoal or grilled as in the recipe. This can be done the day before.

2   Cook the chicken curry direct then indirect.

3   Add the multi-level grid; cook the rice.

4   Prepare the raita.

5   Add the stuffed chillies to the half moon cast-iron searing grid.

NOTES

1   Toast and grind your curry marinade spices in advance; you can use the EGG or kitchen hob for this.

2   If cooking as an entire feast, make sure you have pans that all fit on the EGG at once, otherwise you may need to keep some items warm in an oven.

3   Remember to burp your EGG when opening at high temperatures and cook with the dome closed.

CHICKEN CURRY

Serves 4–6

1 whole chicken, about 2kg/4lb 8oz

2 tsp Tandoori blend powder

1 tsp Kashmiri chilli powder

1 tsp toasted ground coriander

1 tsp toasted ground cumin

1 tsp ground turmeric

1 tsp ground fennel seeds

75g natural (plain) yoghurt

2 onions, thinly sliced

4 garlic cloves, thinly sliced

3 tbsp ghee or neutral oil

2 tsp garam masala

1 tsp ground cumin

½ tsp ground ginger

1 cinnamon stick

2 black cardamom pods, cracked

6 green cardamom pods, cracked

2 cloves

4 whole dried Kashmiri chillies

2 bay leaves

2 tbsp tamarind paste

2 tbsp tomato purée (paste)

3 tomatoes, cut into wedges

Salt and freshly ground black pepper

To serve

1–2 green chillies, thinly sliced

1 tsp garam masala

Bhuna is a Bengali dish created by effectively frying spices in oil to create a flavouring paste in which the meat is then also fried or, you could argue, possibly braised – it's important that the eventual cooking temperature is less than is usually required for pure frying. Remember to burp your EGG when opening at high temperatures and cook with the dome closed.

It's a good idea to get your butcher to spatchcock the chicken, or you can leave it whole, but whatever you do, be sure to slash through the legs to the bone. This speeds the cooking and lets the marinade penetrate. Mix the chicken with the marinade spices (tandoori blend powder, Kashmiri chilli powder, toasted ground coriander and cumin, and ground turmeric and fennel), the yoghurt and ½ teaspoon each of salt and black pepper in a dish and leave to marinate for at least 1 hour.

Meanwhile, in your preheated EGG set up to cook directly, fry the onion and garlic in 1 tablespoon of the ghee or oil in a large cast-iron skillet/pan for 5 minutes until softened, then remove from the heat and blend with ½ teaspoon of salt, the garam masala, ground cumin and ground ginger until you have a smooth paste. Add a splash of water, if necessary.

Fry the whole spices, chillies and bay leaves in the remaining 2 tablespoons of ghee or oil in a wide cast-iron pan for 1 minute until aromatic, then add the onion paste and cook for 5–10 minutes or until all the water has evaporated from the paste and it is beginning to brown on the bottom of the pan.

Add the tamarind paste and tomato purée and cook for 1 minute, then add 300ml/generous 1¼ cups of water, close the dome and bring to the boil, then remove from the EGG.

With heatproof gloves or EGG mitts, change the EGG's set-up from direct to indirect. Once you have reached your target temperature, bake the whole marinated chicken for 40–50 minutes on the grill, with the dome closed, until just about cooked through and nicely coloured.

continued overleaf...

EGG SET UP
Direct set-up, cast-iron pan on the stainless steel grid or cast-iron grid.

Then...
Indirect set-up; the convEGGtor in the legs-up position with the stainless steel grid on top of the convEGGtor legs.

TARGET TEMP
180°C/350°F

Add the chicken to the sauce and cook, uncovered, for a further 20–30 minutes until the chicken is cooked through and the sauce is rich and thick. Keep topping up the pan with water to keep a useful amount of sauce.

Once cooked, remove the chicken from the pan to a plate to rest, then stir the tomato wedges into the curry sauce and cook for 5 minutes with the dome closed, adding a splash of water if you feel you need to.

Return the chicken to the curry sauce and serve topped with the sliced green chillies and the teaspoon of garam masala.

BAKED PILAU

Serves 4

2 large onions, finely sliced

4 tbsp, plus 50g/3½ tbsp ghee or neutral oil

1 cinnamon stick

3 whole cloves

2 bay leaves

10 green cardamom pods, plus 2 black cardamom pods if you can find them, cracked

Pinch of saffron strands

350g/2 cups basmati rice

450ml/2 cups hot water

200ml/scant 1 cup full-fat (whole) milk

Small handful of raisins

50g/generous ½ cup flaked (slivered) almonds, toasted

Salt and freshly ground black pepper

This recipe adopts a technique, common across most rice-growing cultures, of cooking by the absorption method with aromatics in a sealed environment. The rice comes out fluffy, dry and absolutely humming with fragrance. Cooking this way may cause a little of the rice to stick to the bottom of the cooking pot, but most cultures regard this gluey and crisped bit as a positive bonus.

Fry the onions in the 4 tablespoons of ghee or oil in a casserole pan on the hob for about 15 minutes, stirring every 2–3 minutes until soft and starting to brown, then remove 2 tablespoons of the fried onions to a small bowl and set aside.

In another pan on the hob, fry the cinnamon, cloves, bay leaves and cardamom in half the remaining ghee or oil over a moderate heat for 1 minute. Add the saffron and the rice and toast in the ghee/oil and spices for 1 minute more.

Add the hot water and a generous pinch of salt to the rice, bring to the boil on the hob and then cook, uncovered, for 5 minutes until all the water has been absorbed. Remove from the heat and stir in the milk.

Pour the par-cooked rice into an ovenproof dish and dot with the rest of the ghee or drizzle over the remaining oil, then scatter over the raisins and the reserved fried onions. Cover the dish tightly with a lid or foil, burp and open your preheated EGG and cook for 25–30 minutes until the rice is tender.

Burp the EGG, then remove the rice dish and leave to rest for 5 minutes without removing the lid/foil. Serve with the toasted flaked almonds sprinkled on the top.

EGG SET UP
Indirect set-up; the convEGGtor in the legs-up position with the stainless steel grid on top of the convEGGtor legs.

TARGET TEMP
160–180°C/320–350°F

RAITA

Raita is an excellent condiment with curries, but it's really too versatile not to be used elsewhere. Capsaicin is the chemical that 'burns' in spicy food and it's not soluble in water. You can drink as much water or even beer as you like and it won't cool your searing tongue. Yoghurt, though, dissolves the capsaicin and soothes the mouth. That's worth remembering in any cuisine.

Makes 300g/10½oz

½ small red onion, very finely chopped

200g/scant 1 cup natural (plain) yoghurt

Juice of ½ lemon

2 tbsp finely chopped coriander (cilantro)

Pinch of nigella seeds

Salt and freshly ground black pepper

Put the onion in a small dish, sprinkle with a big pinch of salt, rub the salt into the onion and leave for 5 minutes, then rinse with cold water and drain well.

Stir the drained onion into the yoghurt in a bowl along with the lemon juice, half the coriander and the nigella seeds.

Serve topped with the remaining coriander.

STUFFED GREEN CHILLIES

Serves 2–8

½ small red onion, very finely chopped

3 sprigs of coriander (cilantro), finely chopped

1 tbsp vegetable oil

Pinch of salt

1 tsp ground fennel seeds

½ tsp ground coriander

¼ tsp asafoetida powder

1 tsp amchoor (mango powder)

8 green chillies, cut in half lengthways and deseeded

Not all chillies are about heat. Larger green ones have a lovely, fragrant, vegetal quality and a fresh flavour that takes really well to stuffing. Particularly helpful in this case, is amchoor (ground dried green mango), which has a sour note and acts as a foil to the other spices.

Crush the onion and coriander to a very coarse paste using a pestle and mortar, then mix in the vegetable oil, salt, the ground spices, asafoetida and amchoor.

Push this paste into the halved green chillies, dividing it evenly between them, then sandwich the chilli halves together and thread onto two metal skewers to secure.

Burp and open your preheated EGG and grill the stuffed chillies, stuffed-side up, for 2 minutes on each side with the dome closed, until beginning to colour and go tender.

EGG SET UP
Direct set-up with the stainless steel or cast-iron grid.

TARGET TEMP
180°C/350°F

BRINGJAL PICKLE

I'm beginning to think you can never get the really deep flavours out of an aubergine until you've incinerated it. The spongy flesh drinks up aromas so by really scorching it in the heat of the EGG – properly burning the skin – you drive an incredibly complex smokiness right into the flesh. On that base, the spices can go to work, creating a punchy and invigorating pickle. Remember to burp your EGG when opening at high temperatures and cook with the dome closed.

Open your preheated EGG and grill the aubergines for 20 minutes, turning frequently until the skins are really charred and the flesh is very soft.

Open the dome and place your skillet or pan on the grill and fry the sliced onion in the oil for 10 minutes until soft.

Meanwhile, when the aubergines are cool enough to handle, peel them, then roughly chop the flesh.

Add the garlic, ginger, tomatoes, nigella seeds and spices to the cooked onions. Cook for 5 minutes or until the tomatoes have broken down, then stir in the chopped aubergine and cook for 5–8 minutes with the dome closed until the sauce is rich and thick. Remove the pan from the EGG. Add the coriander and lemon juice and season to taste with salt and pepper.

Stored in sterilised jars, the pickle will keep in the fridge for a week.

Makes 2 Jars

3-4 aubergines (eggplants), skin pricked a few times with the point of a knife

1 onion, thinly sliced

2 tbsp oil

4 garlic cloves, finely chopped

2 tbsp finely grated fresh ginger

3 tomatoes, finely chopped

1 tsp nigella seeds

1 tsp kashmiri chilli powder

½ tsp ground turmeric

1 tsp ground coriander

½–1 tsp chilli flakes (red pepper flakes)

½ bunch coriander (cilantro), finely chopped

Juice of ½ lemon

Salt and freshly ground black pepper

EGG SET UP
Direct set-up, with stainless steel or cast-iron grid; you will also need a skillet or a pan that will fit the EGG.

TARGET TEMP
180°C/350°F

MAGHREBI FEAST

The Maghreb is the region of north-west Africa that comprises Libya, Algeria, Morocco and Tunisia, and a variety of cultures and food ways. There's a long coast along the Atlantic and Mediterranean offering amazing seafood and the influences of thousands of years of sea trading and incoming travellers. Through the middle, the Atlas mountains rise, creating areas of great fertility. There are traditions millennia old of preserving fruit by drying, and an age-old spice trade travelling up from nations further south. There are strong traditions of hospitality and group feasting in the area. The 'mechoui', in particular, is a set-piece feast in which a whole sheep or goat is roasted to be shared by the extended family.

SERVES 12–14

FEAST MENU

MECHOUI: Up to 5 hours cooking time 130–150°C/265–300°F then 170–190°C/325–375°F

MATBUCHA: 1 hour cooking time 160–180°C/320–350°F then 130–150°C/265–300°F

COUSCOUS 'ROYALE': 1 hour 40 minutes cooking time 140–160°C/275–320°F then 160–180°C/320–350°F

EZME SALAD: 5–10 minutes cooking 160–180°C/320–350°F

MHADJEB: 30 minutes cooking time 160–180°C/320–350°F

FEAST METHOD
(if cooking everything together as a feast)

1   Cook either the mechoui or couscous 'royale'.

2   Cook the matbucha and ezme salad.

3   Cook the mechoui direct on the half moon cast-iron grid and finish in the paella pan. Remove, add in a plancha or skillet and increase the EGG temperature.

4 Cook the mhadjeb.

EGG FEAST SET UP
(if cooking everything together as a feast)

Load and light your EGG. For the mechoui or couscous bring it to 130°C/265°F and add the convEGGtor basket with the convEGGtor legs up and the stainless steel grid on top.

Then, when cooking the rest of the feast, remove the convEGGtor basket, take out the convEGGtor, add the half moon baking stone bottom left, half moon baking stone top left and the cast-iron searing grid top right.

NOTES

1   If cooking as a feast you will need to make a tough choice on cooking either the mechoui or couscous, as these are large low-and-slow cooks and there's only room for one. Whichever you choose, make sure you have an EGG that has been loaded full with charcoal.

2   If cooking the peppers dirty on the charcoal, make sure you use natural uncoated charcoal like any of the charcoal from the Big Green Egg range, which is made from 100% responsibly sourced hardwood. Secondly, make sure a large enough surface area of the charcoal is smouldering or white; you do not need all the charcoal to be white to cook on it.

3   If cooking the mhadjeb and you don't have a plancha or cast-iron skillet, you could use a preheated baking stone.

MECHOUI

For the nomadic groups of the Sahara, sheep and goats are really the only acceptable form of portable livestock, as they are able to move with the families, transported by camel, horse and mule, in search of water and grazing. Families naturally eat together and meals are shaped by the restrictions and concerns of weight and portability. Meals often centre on rice or couscous – easy to pack and carry while dry – and an animal slaughtered from the flock. Groups often eat, using their hands, from a central shared plate or metal tray – lighter to carry than individual crockery. One could even argue that they favour spices where the smallest amount packs the mightiest punch. In this recipe, we specify the constituent parts of half a lamb, which will serve 10 hungry people while being manageable to handle. You can easily scale up or down so chose your cuts of meat depending on the size of EGG you're working with and the number of guests. Remember to burp your EGG when opening at high temperatures and cook with the dome closed.

EGG SET UP
Indirect set-up; the convEGGtor in the legs-up position with the stainless steel grid or cast-iron grid on top of the legs, or the baking stone in place.
TARGET TEMP
130–150°C/265–300°F

Then...
Direct set-up, with the stainless steel or cast-iron grid with a paella pan sitting on top.
TARGET TEMP
170–190°C/325–375°F

2 tbsp ground cumin

1 tbsp ground cinnamon

½ tsp freshly ground black pepper

Big pinch of saffron strands

8 garlic cloves, crushed

200g/generous ¾ cup butter, softened

1 leg of lamb

1 shoulder of lamb

1 rack of lamb

2 lamb's kidneys, cleaned, trimmed and cut into quarters

1 lamb's heart, cleaned, trimmed and cut into quarters

For the rice

3 tbsp olive oil, plus extra for greasing

500g/1lb 2oz Bomba rice

1L/4⅓ cups chicken stock or water

Pinch of saffron strands

Salt

Combine the ground spices, saffron, garlic and butter in a bowl to form a rub. Rub half of this all over the whole pieces of lamb (leg, shoulder and rack). Set the remainder aside.

Using the indirect set-up, oil the grill lightly and then place the whole pieces of lamb on the grill. Close the dome and cook for around 1½–2 hours until the spices have formed a crust.

Move the meat to a roasting tray and brush with the remaining butter rub, then wrap in butcher's paper (or baking paper) or double wrap in foil. Return to the grill for a further 1½–2½ hours until the meat is meltingly tender and the bones easily slide away from the meat.

Remove the meat from the EGG, place in a clean roasting tray, then cover with foil and leave to rest for at least 30 minutes.

Meanwhile, thread the offal onto metal skewers.

Using the direct set-up for the rice, heat the paella pan in the EGG.

Add the olive oil to the pan and toast the rice for a few minutes, then add the stock or water and saffron and bring the pan to a simmer. Add salt to taste and shake the pan gently as you do, so that the mixture evens out.

Close the dome and let the rice cook for about 20–30 minutes or until the rice is just cooked and the liquid has been fully absorbed.

Remove from the EGG, cover with foil and rest for at least 10 minutes, fluffing it up to serve.

While the rice rests, grill the offal skewers, turning once for 2-3 minutes on each side, and serve on top of the rice with the large pieces of meat.

MATBUCHA

Serves 6

2 red (bell) peppers

1kg/2lb 4oz plum tomatoes

4 garlic cloves, finely chopped

120ml/½ cup neutral oil

15g/½oz sweet paprika

5g/⅙oz chilli flakes (red pepper flakes)

Salt

Matbucha is a tomato and pepper dip. There are similar preparations in different parts of the Mediterranean, but this Moroccan version seems to have the best combination of sweetness, sourness and gentle peppery heat. Whenever I put this out on a table, it takes people a while to notice it – it just looks like lumpy ketchup – but then from the moment the first flatbread gets dipped in, it's usually just minutes before it's all gone and guests are fighting for the last smears in the bowl.

Using the direct set-up, burp and open your preheated EGG and burn the peppers black (all over) on the grill bars of the EGG (or directly in the coals), with the dome closed, turning, for 5–10 minutes. Transfer them (while hot) to a heatproof bowl or suitable plastic container and cover. The scorching and steam will make the skins easy to strip off and add a smoky taste. (Do this at the same time as the peppers for the salad on page 86.)

Peel, deseed and coarsely chop the peppers, and peel, core and chop the tomatoes. Place both in a large pan with the garlic, oil, paprika and chilli flakes.

Using the indirect set-up, burp the EGG and place the pan on the stainless steel grid. Stew down the pepper/tomato mixture over a low heat for an hour or so, with the dome closed, until jammy.

Season with salt after you've reduced the mixture and achieved the right consistency. If you season earlier, the reduction will concentrate the salt, with unpleasant results.

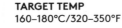

EGG SET UP
Direct set-up with the stainless steel grid or cast-iron grid.

TARGET TEMP
160–180°C/320–350°F

Then...
Indirect set-up; the convEGGtor in the legs-up position with the stainless steel grid on top of the convEGGtor legs.

TARGET TEMP
130–150°C/265–300°F

COUSCOUS 'ROYALE'

France has a long and complicated colonial history in the Maghreb, much as the British have in India. Where we have adopted and adapted curries as our own, the French have thoroughly embraced couscous – effectively a 'pasta' of grainy pellets made from semolina flour (cream of wheat). The best expression of couscous, popular in brasseries and restaurants all over France and in French tourist hotels across the Maghreb, is the couscous 'Royale' – officially defined as containing three meats, vegetables, chickpeas (garbanzo beans) and even hard-boiled eggs (the latter always feels a step too far for me). This dish is an absolute feast in itself, as you serve several courses from the same shared dish. With all the formality of traditional restaurants, it's easy to see how the relaxed, companionable sharing of couscous 'Royale' must have appealed to French diners. It's not really very 'authentic', perhaps in the same way as British 'curry', but it's created its own story. Remember to burp your EGG when opening at high temperatures and cook with the dome closed.

FOR THE LAMB AND THE VEG

Using the direct set-up, open your preheated EGG and cook the onion, carrots and celery in the olive oil in a large skillet or pan for 5 minutes, with the dome closed, then stir in the garlic, parsley, chilli flakes, saffron strands, cinnamon sticks, bay leaves and ground ginger and cook for 1 minute until fragrant.

Now change the set ups from direct to indirect in the EGG. Add the tomato purée and let it cook for another minute, then add the lamb and cook for 5 minutes to combine. Add the stock and then cook, uncovered, for 40 minutes.

Stir in the canned tomatoes and chickpeas, the sultanas and preserved lemon and cook, covered, for 20 minutes, then finally add the turnips and courgette. Season with salt and pepper, then cook covered for a further 25–30 minutes until all the vegetables and the lamb are tender.

Strain and separate the lamb, vegetables and cooking broth into three separate bowls. Remove the cinnamon sticks and bay leaves.

Serves 6–8

For the lamb and the veg
1 onion, cut into 8 wedges

2 carrots, cut into 5cm/2in pieces

2 celery sticks, cut into 5cm/2in pieces

50ml/scant ¼ cup olive oil

4 garlic cloves, sliced

Bunch of flat-leaf parsley, roughly chopped

Good pinch of chilli flakes (red pepper flakes)

Large pinch of saffron strands

2 cinnamon sticks

2 bay leaves

2g/¹⁄₁₆oz ground ginger

30g/1oz tomato purée (paste)

500g/1lb 2oz boneless shoulder of lamb, diced

1L/4⅓ cups chicken stock

1 x 400g/14oz can chopped tomatoes

1 x 400g/14oz can chickpeas (garbanzo beans), drained and rinsed

100g/¾ cup sultanas (golden raisins)

1 preserved lemon, finely chopped

4 baby turnips

1 courgette (zucchini), cut into 5cm/2in pieces

Salt and freshly ground black pepper

Harissa, to serve

For the couscous and chicken mix
350g/2 cups quick-cook couscous

250ml/generous 1 cup boiling water

40g/3 tbsp butter

500g/1lb 2oz skinless, boneless chicken thighs

50ml/scant ¼ cup olive oil

8 Merguez sausages

1 onion, thinly sliced

6 garlic cloves, thinly sliced

2 tsp ground cumin

Bunch of coriander (cilantro), roughly chopped

Salt and freshly ground black pepper

EGG SET UP
Direct set-up with stainless steel or cast-iron grid (cooking direct to start with to cook down the onions; target temp should be about 140–160°C, to match the indirect cooking next).

Then...
Indirect set-up – the plate setter in the legs up position with the stainless steel grid on top of the plate setter legs (to braise the meat and vegetables).

TARGET TEMP
140–160°C/275–320°F

Then...

EGG SET UP
Direct set-up with stainless steel or cast-iron grid (to cook the sausage and chicken and sauté the vegetables).

TARGET TEMP
160–180°C/320–350°F

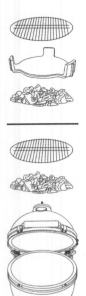

FOR THE COUSCOUS AND THE CHICKEN MIX

While the lamb and veg are cooking, prepare the couscous. Put the couscous into a large heatproof bowl, then stir in the boiling water, adding the butter and some salt. Cover with a clean, damp dish towel and set aside for 5 minutes. Uncover and use a fork and clean fingers to break/fluff up the grains. Taste again for seasoning.

Meanwhile, using the direct set-up in the EGG, in a frying pan, brown the chicken pieces in the olive oil until brown, then add the Merguez sausages and cook for 5 minutes.

Add the onion, garlic and cumin with some salt and pepper, then cover and cook for 20 minutes until the chicken is cooked, stirring every now and then. Stir in the coriander.

TO ASSEMBLE

Use a large serving platter to serve (use a heatproof one, if you want to return it to the EGG). Spread the couscous out over the plate or platter and make a large indent in the middle.

Put the lamb and the chicken mix in the middle.

Top with the vegetable mixture, arranging the vegetables as you wish.

Divide the cooking broth into two separate serving bowls, stirring harissa to taste into one of them. Serve the broth on the side and ladle over.

EZME SALAD

Serves 4–6 as a side

2 large red (bell) peppers

500g/1lb 2oz tomatoes

1 large onion, minced

2 garlic cloves, finely chopped

2 hot green jalapeño chilli peppers, finely chopped and deseeded

½ tsp salt, plus extra for seasoning

25g/1oz parsley, finely chopped

Pinch of dried mint

Pinch of chilli flakes (red pepper flakes)

3g/⅟₁₆ oz ground sumac

3 tbsp olive oil

Juice of a lemon

25g/1oz pomegranate molasses

The first time I ate Ezme Salad was in Paris. I couldn't believe I'd never experienced it before. I'm sure my brain was addled by the romance of the city, but it just seemed I'd never encountered anything so fresh and that played so well with hot/sour/sweet. Most original Turkish recipes don't include the sweet red (bell) peppers, but then most Turkish recipes are based around some of the most legendary delicious tomatoes in the world. The red peppers we can buy today are exceptionally sweet, an effect that's enhanced by flame-roasting them.

Burp and open your preheated EGG and burn the peppers black (all over) on the grill bars (or directly in the coals), turning, for 5–10 minutes, then transfer them (while hot) to a heatproof bowl or suitable plastic container and cover. The scorching and steam will make the skins easy to strip off and add a smoky taste.

Prep your tomatoes. If you're fussy, you can remove and discard the seeds, but if you do you'll need to increase your total quantity to around 750g/1lb 10oz. Do, however, be sure to remove any tough cores up around the stems. Chop the flesh into fine dice. Remove the seeds and stems from the peeled, roasted red peppers, then chop the flesh into fine dice.

Place the onion, garlic and jalapeño chilli peppers in a bowl with the measured salt, then, wearing disposable gloves, grind everything together between your hands. The salt cuts up the cells of the veg, allowing the most acrid bits of the onion and garlic to evaporate, and releasing the heat from the jalapeños.

While you have your gloves on, add the parsley and mint and scrunch them up too. The salt will help release the flavours.

Add the tomatoes and grilled peppers to the crushed onion mixture and season with the chilli flakes, sumac and some more salt if necessary.

Whisk together the olive oil, lemon juice and pomegranate molasses, then add to the salad and toss to mix. Leave to stand for an hour or so at room temperature before serving.

EGG SET UP
Direct set-up with the stainless steel grid or cast-iron grid.

TARGET TEMP
160–180°C/320–350°F

MHADJEB

Mhadjeb is a popular street food in Algeria, a flatbread which, rather than using a leavening agent to make it rise, is made light by lamination. By using incredibly strong, high gluten semolina flour (cream of wheat), it's possible to hand-stretch a dough that's thin enough to read the paper through. This is then oiled and folded into layers that puff up when the bread hits the hotplate. In this recipe, we've added a little tomato stuffing, but you could also add ricotta and spinach, spiced minced meat or perhaps stewed mushrooms.

Place the semolina in a bowl, stir in the measured salt, then add water a spoonful at a time, kneading until you achieve a hard but cohesive dough. Knead until smooth. Cover and rest for an hour or so.

Burp and open your preheated EGG. In a large skillet or pan, sweat down the onions, chillies, carrot and garlic in a splash of the olive oil until dark and jammy, about 10–15 minutes. Crush the canned tomatoes, then add to the mix and cook, wth the dome closed, until reduced and thickened, about 8–10 minutes. Season with salt and pepper, then stir in the chilli flakes and coriander.

Cut the semolina dough into golf-ball sized pieces. On an oiled surface (marble or silpat) push out each ball of dough and flatten it into a disc, then roll and stretch the dough with oiled hands until it is very thin and transparent. Keep your hands and the surface well oiled.

Smear a tablespoon of the tomato filling into the centre of each disc, then fold over two sides, 'letter'-style, so it is three layers thick. Then letter-fold again in the other direction, so it is nine layers thick.

Burp and open the preheated EGG and cook the mhadjeb seam-side down on the plancha or in a large, cast-iron skillet for a minute or so, flipping them to crisp the tops.

Makes 4

200g/1⅓ cups fine semolina

1½ tsp salt, plus extra for seasoning

2 onions, finely chopped

3 red chillies, finely chopped

1 carrot, peeled and grated

3 garlic cloves, crushed

100ml/½ cup olive oil

1 x 400g/14oz can whole peeled plum tomatoes in juice

10g/¼oz chilli flakes (red pepper flakes)

Bunch of coriander (cilantro), roughly chopped

Freshly ground black pepper

EGG SET UP
Direct set-up with the stainless steel grid, plus the plancha or a large, cast-iron skillet.

TARGET TEMP
160–180°C/320–350°F

TUSCAN FEAST

We may not all be lucky enough to eat in Tuscany very often but many of us look to the region as the spiritual home of large-scale, outdoor feasting. It's the combination of astonishing local ingredients, ideal mellow weather and almost certainly the phenomenal light and landscape which have made Tuscany the location for countless feasts in photographs and film.

We can't always have a loggia, draped in bougainvillea, to hand, with a view over rolling hills to the duomo glinting in the distance. Your backyard, like mine, might be a little light on honeyed stone and statuary, but that doesn't mean we can't put a little work into set dressing. How would Coppola or Scorsese have approached this? Probably a white tablecloth, definitely some fairy lights. Red wine looks great in rustic tumblers rather than the posh glassware, and be sure to cast the whole family. You need grandparents at the table as well as photogenic children running around.

With the cast and the set organized, the single most important ingredient in Tuscan eating is time. Thousands of years of history in the ingredients and recipes, unhurried and careful cooking, but most of all, allowing yourself time to appreciate what's being served. Italian meals are long affairs, usually with a starter, a pasta course, something grilled, and desserts, not to mention breads and salads. There are always spare things to pick at. You might not need all of these, but do plan to stretch the courses apart. Why rush? You need time to discuss, to gossip, to plot, to decide which of the heads of the Five Families you're going to have assassinated. Okay, maybe not that last one, but certainly plan to start in a leisurely way in the mid-afternoon and don't expect to get up from the table 'til midnight.

Rustic Italian cooking involves grilling over wood or charcoal, and a lot of slow roasting in clay ovens. Both are ideal to replicate with the EGG. Unlike, say, Southern US cooking, there's not much requirement for heavy smoke flavours, but subtle scorching and just enough smoke to remind you that it was done with live fire, are the keys.

This feast is inspired by the Bistecca Fiorentina, a mighty piece of meat taken from a particular and ancient breed of draught cattle. There's something especially appealing about cooking one vast steak and sharing it. It's worth making an effort to source the best cut from the best carcass your butcher can manage. Because it's going to be shared, less will be needed and less will be wasted. It's more congenial, usually works out to be more economical and really bears out the wisdom of serving less but higher-quality meat.

SERVES 6–8

FEAST MENU

**SQUID STUFFED WITH
FENNEL SAUSAGE:** 15 minutes
cooking time 160–180°C/320–350°F

'FLORENTINE STEAK: cooking time
depends on how you like your steak
220–260°C/425–500°F

PORCINI BUTTER

CELERY AND ENDIVE GRATIN:
40 minutes cooking time
200–220°C/400–425°F

ROSEMARY AND GARLIC POTATOES:
15 minutes cooking time
200°C/400°F

EGG FEAST SET UP
(if cooking everything together as
a feast)

Load and light your EGG. Bring
it to 180°C/350°F and add the
convEGGtor basket with half moon
baking stones bottom left and right,
stainless steel grids top left and top
right, then, when needed, remove
the right-hand stainless steel grid
and half moon baking stone and
add in the half moon cast-iron
searing grid on the top right, with
the multi-level grid.

FEAST METHOD
(if cooking everything together as a feast)

1   Prepare the squid.

2   Make the porcini butter.

3   Start the potatoes.

4   Ten minutes in, start the celery and
    endive gratin.

5   After about 30 minutes, take out one
    baking stone and stainless steel grid and
    replace with a half moon cast-iron searing
    grid, and add the multi-level rack.

6   Increase the temperature to 250–270°C/
    480–520°F.

7   Have the celery and endive gratin at the
    top, the potatoes over the baking stone
    side and cook the steak on the cast-iron
    searing grid side.

8   Rest the steak while you cook the squid
    stuffed with fennel sausage and the
    potatoes.

NOTES

1   When loading and lighting the EGG, you
    must be generous with the charcoal; this is
    not the time to be frugal. You will need a
    healthy amount of charcoal to reach and
    sustain the high temperatures needed to
    cook the steak.

2   Remember to burp your EGG when opening
    at high temperatures and cook with the
    dome closed.

3   Master temperature control. Take your time
    when increasing your temperature from
    180°C/350°F to 270°C/520°F when cooking
    the steak. It will be difficult to bring the
    temperature down if it gets carried away
    beyond the 300°C/570°F mark.

4   Make sure you use a digital thermometer
    to take the internal reading of the steak to
    how you like it. Nothing worse than sad
    faces eating steak.

5   Rest the steak well before serving, it is a
    balance though, as you do not want to
    serve it cold.

SQUID STUFFED WITH FENNEL SAUSAGE

Serves 4

For the filling

350g/12oz Tuscan fennel salsicce (or use 300g/10½oz plain pork sausagemeat, combined with 50g/1¾oz finocchiona, finely chopped, and a pinch of whole fennel seeds)

1 tsp ground fennel seeds

2 large garlic cloves, crushed

Salt and freshly ground black pepper

To stuff and serve

12 small (9–12cm/3½–4½in) squid bodies, plus tentacles if they have them, cleaned

Olive oil, for brushing and drizzling

A few sprigs of flat-leaf parsley, finely chopped

Pinch of chilli flakes (red pepper flakes)

Combining pork and fish may be a little counter-intuitive to western palates, but it's one of the great things we've learned from South Asian cuisine. The highly flavoured fennel pork sausage and squid are both Italian favourites, so why not bring them together?

For the filling, remove the skins from the salsicce (if using). Mix the filling ingredients together in a bowl until well mixed, adding salt and pepper to taste.

Chop the squid tentacles (if using) and add them to the sausage filling mix.

Use a teaspoon to stuff the squid bodies with the filling mixture, leaving 1cm/½in empty at the top of each. Close the open end of each with a cocktail stick/toothpick.

Place on a plate and refrigerate for 1 hour.

Place the squid in a pan of cold salted water ensuring there is enough water to completely cover.

Place on the hob and bring to the boil, then reduce to a gentle simmer for 8-10 minutes and drain on a clean tea towel.

Leave to cool, then refrigerate until ready to grill.

When ready to grill, brush the stuffed squid all over with a little olive oil. Burp and open your preheated EGG, then grill for 5–7 minutes, with the dome closed, turning until golden in places.

Serve drizzled with more olive oil and tossed with the parsley and chilli flakes.

EGG SET UP
Direct set-up with the plancha or stainless steel grid or cast-iron searing grid in place (to serve).

TARGET TEMP
160–180°C/320–350°F

'FLORENTINE' STEAK

Serves 4–6

1 T-bone steak about 800g–1kg/
1lb 12oz–2lb 4oz

Flaky sea salt or fleur de sel

Coarsely ground black pepper

Steak cooking times can vary
depending on the thickness of the
steak and the cooking temperature,
so it's useful to understand internal
temperatures. The meat will
continue to cook as it rests, so use
the guidelines below to know when
to remove from the grid.

**Internal temperatures to remove
from the grid:**

Rare: 45–48°C/113–118°F, to serve
about 50°C/122°F

Medium-rare: 50–52°C/122–126°F,
to serve about 55°C/131°F

Medium: 55–58°C/131–136°F, to serve
about 60°C/140°F

Medium-well: 60–63°C/140–145°F,
to serve about 65°C/149°F

Well-done: 68–70°C+/154–158°F+,
to serve 70°C+/158°F+

A proper Bistecca Fiorentina is taken from the Chianina
draught cattle native to Tuscany. It's a Porterhouse cut,
so effectively a T-bone taken from the thick end. This
means that there is substantial sirloin and fillet on either
side of the main bone. It's a spectacular cut, rare and
expensive, but there's no reason why you shouldn't cook
a more regular T-bone the same way. The key thing is the
thickness. In Florence, they say a bistecca should be as
thick as the length of a matchstick.

Season the steak generously with salt (searing steak with
pepper turns it bitter and burns; just salt the night before,
which caramelizes and creates the perfect crust, the Maillard
reaction) – preferably the night before you intend to cook.
Refrigerate it uncovered and standing upright on the bone.
This will dry the surface of the meat for a crisp crust.

Bring the steak up to room temperature before cooking.
Preheat the EGG, with the cast-iron or stainless steel grid.

Burp and open the EGG. Start by pressing the fat edge, if
the steak has one, onto the grid until browned, then move
to the flesh side. Cook, with the dome closed, for about
2–3 minutes on each side, pressing down, until both sides
are very nicely browned.

Turn the steak every minute until it's done to your liking.
Season with pepper. See cooking times and internal
temperatures on the left.

Allow the steak to rest somewhere warm for 20 minutes,
with a big blob of the porcini butter.

Slice off the bone, then slice the steak into 1.5–2cm/⅝–¾in
slices, adding more porcini butter.

EGG SET UP
Direct set-up with
the stainless steel
grid or cast-iron
grid on top.

TARGET TEMP
220–260°C/425–
500°F

PORCINI BUTTER

Makes around 150g/5½oz

20g/¾oz dried porcini mushrooms, rinsed and soaked in 100ml/scant ½ cup boiling water for 5 minutes

100g/7 tbsp butter, softened

2 garlic cloves, peeled

1 tsp thyme leaves

Salt and freshly ground black pepper

Flavoured butters are the perfect accompaniment to a grand steak, and especially porcini with its rich, dark, forest-floor flavours. The trick here is getting the two to combine. Too much of the highly flavoured soaking liquid will make the butter 'split' when it comes out of the fridge, so this technique removes all the excess moisture after the mushrooms are reconstituted and uses melted butter to 'deglaze' the pan. This can easily be made in a hot EGG (220°C/425°F) set up for direct cooking, or on a hob.

Drain and finely chop the mushrooms, reserving the soaking liquid. Strain the soaking liquid into a small pan, then bubble until it's reduced as far as you dare... to a syrup and a little beyond until it's almost dry on the bottom of the pan, then add a little of the butter and scrape everything up. You want to get every bit of mushroom flavour into the butter.

Grate the garlic into the melted butter and cook gently until it softens, about 1 minute.

Remove from the heat, allow the butter in the pan to cool, then mix it into the remaining butter along with the chopped mushrooms, stirring in the thyme leaves at the end. Season with salt and pepper.

CELERY AND ENDIVE GRATIN

Serves 4

6 endives, quartered (or use 3 radicchio, thickly sliced)

1 tbsp olive oil

4 thin slices of prosciutto or pancetta, each cut into four

5 celery sticks, thinly sliced on an angle

1 onion, thinly sliced

200ml/scant 1 cup double (heavy) cream

Handful of grated Parmesan cheese

Handful of panko breadcrumbs

Salt and freshly ground black pepper

The enclosed cooking environment of the EGG makes it absolutely ideal for vegetable gratins. Vegetables are braised in a little liquid (if necessary, cover with foil so tougher veg steam through), then add cream and even cheese to the liquid and cook, uncovered, until a delicious crust forms. Both the celery and endive give up delicious juices when cooked so are ideal for this method. Remember to burp your EGG when cooking at high temperatures.

Open the preheated EGG and grill the endives for about 8 minutes with the dome closed, turning a few times, until golden and softened, adding salt and pepper to taste. Remove from the EGG and set aside.

Open the EGG again and heat the oil in a shallow pan, then add the prosciutto or pancetta. Add the celery and onion and cook for 5 minutes with the dome closed.

Open the EGG, add the grilled endives to the pan and stir well, then stir in the cream and top with the Parmesan and breadcrumbs.

Open the EGG, remove the grid, put the convEGGtor in an indirect position with the stainless steel grid and bake with the dome closed for 20 minutes until golden brown.

EGG SET UP
Direct set-up with the stainless steel grid or cast-iron searing grid in place.

Then...
Indirect set-up; the convEGGtor in the legs-up position with the stainless steel grid on top of the convEGGtor legs.

TARGET TEMP
200–220°C/400–425°F

ROSEMARY AND GARLIC POTATOES

Serves 6–8 as as side

1kg/2lb 4oz waxy potatoes, peeled and thickly sliced

30g/2 tbsp butter, softened

1 sprig of rosemary, leaves picked and finely chopped

2 garlic cloves, crushed or finely grated

4–5 tbsp beef dripping or olive oil

Salt and freshly ground black pepper

Potatoes can seem like a heavy, wintry starch so it's a challenge to cook them appropriately for summer. These garlicky, herby little numbers are irresistible and seem to sit perfectly next to a well-rested steak, straight from the EGG. Have these boiled and the butter made, then finish while the steak is resting.

Boil the potatoes in a pan of salted water until tender, then drain well and leave to cool a little. Spread out on a tray on a clean dish towel to dry.

Mix the butter with the rosemary and garlic in a small dish and set aside.

Burp and open your preheated EGG, drizzle 3 tablespoons of the dripping or oil into the cast-iron pan, then place the potato slices, cut-side down, in the pan and cook until deep golden brown on both sides, adding another tablespoon or so of fat, if required. This will take 10–15 minutes with the dome closed.

Once crispy, burp the EGG and stir through the rosemary and garlic butter; cook for a minute or so, adding salt and pepper to taste, then serve.

EGG SET UP
Indirect set-up; the convEGGtor in the legs-up position with the stainless steel grid on top of the convEGGtor legs, with a cast-iron pan on top.

TARGET TEMP
200°C/400°F

SEAFOOD PARTY

It's been established through archaeological evidence that some of the earliest food that humans cooked was shellfish. Long before we had pots or vessels with which to boil, we somehow discovered that shellfish could be placed in fire embers and would steam beautifully in their own juices. There are still varied and exciting traditions of seafood cooking all around the world. In the States, clams or lobsters are steamed, wrapped in wet sacking and seaweed, and buried in a hole in the beach in which a fire has been set. The same pit-cooking method appears as Hangi in Aotearoa or as part of a traditional Lū'au in Hawaii. This technique is easy to replicate in an EGG, where the closed dome ensures no steam is lost.

Most keen outdoor cooks are at ease with grilling seafood. The contact between the bars and scales, skin or shell, creates a very special palette of flavours, but, with the exception of the bread, all of these recipes to some extent use trapped and controlled steam to do the cooking work. The grill flavour is lost, but more subtle flavours of seawater and seaweed can then predominate.

Tearing into a big, cracked crab is very much outdoor business. Things tend to get messy and there's a lot of collateral debris to be disposed of, but both the scallop and the oyster recipes are simple to cook and look sensational at the table. I have my EGGs in the UK where we have oyster and scallop seasons through the winter, so I often do these two, wrapped up in a big coat outside the kitchen door, then bring them in to an appreciative crowd.

EGG FEAST SET UP
(if cooking everything together as a feast)

Load and light your EGG. Bring it to 200°C/ 400°F and add the full moon stainless steel grid or full cast-iron searing grid direct over the charcoal on a convEGGtor basket. You will also need an EGGspander system multi-level grid.

FEAST METHOD
(if cooking everything together as a feast)

1   Make the cockle butter.

2   Cook the potatoes in a skillet on the full moon stainless steel grid, then remove and keep warm.

3   Cook the crab boil on the grill, and serve.

4   Add the multi-level grid. Cook the loaves in a skillet on the full moon stainless steel grid. Once puffed up, move up to the multi-level grid. Serve.

5   Grill the oysters and scallops directly on the full moon stainless steel grid.

NOTES

1   You will be cooking solely directly for this feast; grilling over the charcoal and direct in a hot skillet. Keep an eye on the loaves, as you do not want the bottoms to burn in the skillet if it gets too hot.

2   Remember to burp your EGG when opening at high temperatures and cook with the dome closed.

3   You can cook and serve this feast in stages: cook, serve, demolish, next course.

SERVES 6–12

FEAST MENU
COCKLE LOAVES:
3–7 minutes cooking time depending on temperature 250–280°C/ 480–530°F (direct set-up)

SALT WATER CRUST POTATOES:
45 minutes cooking time
220°C/425°F

CRAB BOIL:
15–20 minutes cooking time
200°C/400°F

OYSTERS:
3–5 minutes cooking time
260°C/500°F

LUTED SCALLOPS:
3–5 minutes cooking time
260°C/500°F

COCKLE LOAVES

Little loaves that have been cooked with a big lump of flavoured butter on top should probably have a separate name all of their own. Somehow the flavourings penetrate each loaf as it cooks, the top crust half-fries and the entire thing is gloriously indulgent. Particularly good for dipping into brown crabmeat.

For the butter, you can use cockles that have been cooked in the jar for this recipe, but I buy fresh (shelled) cockles whenever I'm at the seaside and freeze them spread out on a tray. I then store them loose in a bag so I can grab a handful whenever I feel the need to boost fish or add to these loaves.

Add the yeast to the water in a bowl and stir until the yeast is dissolved. Mix the yeast mixture into the flour in a large bowl until completely combined into a dough. Cover and leave to rest for 10 minutes. Fold in the salt using your hands, then cover and leave for 10 minutes more. Fold the dough one more time, then cover and leave to stand in a warm place for 30–60 minutes until doubled in size.

Have a pizza peel or thin boards ready and dust lightly with flour. Divide the dough into four pieces, shape into rolls, then cover with a damp dish towel and leave to rise again in a warm place.

Meanwhile, for the butter, beat the cockles into the butter along with the shallot, thyme and some salt and pepper and mix well. Transfer to a serving bowl, cover and keep soft at room temperature.

When ready to cook, 'punch down' the centre of each 'loaf' a little to create an indentation into which the butter can be dropped.

Move one onto the peel and top with about a quarter of the softened cockle butter. Burp and open the preheated EGG. Slide onto the hot skillet and cook for 3 minutes or until puffed up and slightly charred on the bottom and sizzling on top (this really does depend on the temperature – as you open and close the EGG, the temperature can rise quite quickly). Halfway through cooking, use a brush to spread some of the butter over the upper crust.

Slide the cooked loaf onto a chopping board and then repeat with the remaining dough balls and butter, eating them as soon as possible. (Your mother probably told you that eating hot bread would give you indigestion. She was wrong.)

Makes 4

7g/⅛oz dried yeast

350ml/1½ cups tepid water

500g/3½ cups white bread flour, plus extra for dusting

½ teaspoon salt

150g/⅔ cup cockle butter (see below)

For the cockle butter filling (Makes about 200g/7oz)

75g/2¾oz (shelled) cockles, roughly chopped

100g/7 tbsp salted butter, cut into cubes and softened

½ shallot, finely chopped

1–2 tsp thyme leaves, roughly chopped

Salt and coarsely ground black pepper

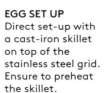

EGG SET UP
Direct set-up with a cast-iron skillet on top of the stainless steel grid. Ensure to preheat the skillet.

TARGET TEMP
250–280°C/480–530°F

SALT WATER CRUST POTATOES

Serves 6–8 as a side

1kg/2lb 4oz small new potatoes, scrubbed, rinsed and left unpeeled

120g/4¼oz coarse salt

3 bay leaves

Coarsest ground black pepper

Butter and freshly chopped herbs, to serve

The EGG favours this cooking method of steaming veg. Because of its unique closed cooking environment, it's possible to control evaporation so the veg are perfectly cooked as the liquid cooks off, leaving any flavourings to coat the food. These potatoes end up as salty as crisps, but they're amazing, in moderation, with seafood.

Place the potatoes, salt and bay leaves in a single layer in a tray or large cast-iron pan, add enough water to half the depth of the potatoes and stir to dissolve the salt.

Burp and open the preheated EGG, and cook the potatoes, with the dome closed, rolling them around occasionally, until the liquid has evaporated and the potatoes are covered in a film of salt, about 45 minutes.

Remove from the EGG and let the potatoes rest for 5 minutes in the pan, uncovered, then season with black pepper. Serve with butter and herbs.

EGG SET UP
Direct set-up with the stainless steel grid or cast-iron grid, and with a large cast-iron pan or skillet on top.

TARGET TEMP
220°C/425°F

CRAB BOIL

Serves 6–8

2 large brown or spider crabs

Beer of your choice (optional)

20g/¾oz seasoning mix (see below)

A few big handfuls of kelp, either fresh or dried (if dried, rinse in water for a few minutes, then drain)

For the seasoning mix
(Make this mix in larger quantities as it stores well in an airtight container, but start with a pinch of each ingredient and play it by ear.)

Grind together (either in a spice grinder or using a pestle and mortar) equal quantities of...

Smoked paprika

Garlic powder

Celery seeds

Ground white pepper

Dried oregano

Cayenne pepper

Dried thyme

English mustard powder

Plus a half quantity of star anise seeds and grated zest of 1 lemon

To serve
Lemon wedges

Crab picks or small spoons or forks

In the American South, a crab 'boil' is usually done with lots of small 'blue' crabs or even freshwater crayfish but up on the North Eastern seaboard they favour lobsters and 'Dungeness' crabs, what we in the UK call brown crab. With this method of cooking we replicate a 'clam bake' with trapped steam flavoured with seaweed. This is even better if you can find yourself a bucket of seawater as the base of your boiling liquid.

Your fishmonger will kill your crabs for you; otherwise use whichever method you find acceptable.

Pour beer (if using) or water into a large cast-iron pot to a depth of about 5cm/2in. Add half the seasoning mix. Create a bed of kelp (keeping some back for the top layer) in the liquid and lay the crabs on it.

Dust the crabs with the rest of the seasoning mix and add another layer of kelp. Put the lid on the pot.

Burp and open the preheated EGG and add the pot. Bring to the boil. Steam for 20–25 minutes, depending on the size of the crabs, with the dome closed. The crabs are cooked when you can easily pull off a claw.

Taking care of the very hot steam, lift out the crabs and place on a large tray.

Lay each crab on its back and twist off the legs and claws. Separate the claw sections, then carefully crack the claws (trying not to shatter them) with the back of a heavy knife or a hammer and place on a serving platter.

Use a cloth to hold the shell and pull the body section out. Loosen the brown meat in the shells and stir it with a fork. Place the shells with the brown meat on the platter.

Remove the 'dead man's fingers' from the core.

Cut the core in half with a sharp knife and add to the platter.

Note: Live crabs should be stored in the bottom of the fridge, covered with a damp dish towel to keep them sedated until ready to kill and cook.

EGG SET UP
Direct set-up with the stainless steel grid or cast-iron grid, and a large cast-iron Dutch oven with a lid on top.

TARGET TEMP
200°C/400°F

OYSTERS

To my eternal unhappiness, I'm somehow allergic to raw oysters, but grilling means I can eat them with joy. A shucked oyster contains enough seawater to steam in and a little strip of nori seaweed adds to the salty tang. The idea here is not to cook the life out of the oysters so much as to 'set ' them.

Shuck the oysters and transfer them to a small bowl, along with all the liquids. Scrub and rinse the shells.

Wrap one strip of seaweed around each oyster, then return each oyster to its shell. Strain the collected liquid and distribute back over the oysters.

Mix the shallot, vinegar or lemon juice and finely chopped seaweed with some black pepper in a small bowl and set aside.

Burp and open the preheated EGG and grill the oysters without turning, until just steamed, about 3–5 minutes.

Arrange the oysters on a serving platter and top each with a dash or two of the shallot dressing. Serve immediately.

Serves 6–12 as an appetizer

12 fresh oysters in shell

1 sheet of nori, 12 strips cut from one half, the remaining finely chopped

½ shallot, very finely chopped

2 tbsp white wine vinegar or lemon juice

Freshly ground black pepper

EGG SET UP
Direct set-up with the stainless steel grid or cast-iron grid on top.

TARGET TEMP
260°C/500°F

LUTED SCALLOPS

We can extend the idea of steaming shellfish in their juices by using a medieval technique called 'luting' – sealing the shells closed with a flour and water paste so the steam can't escape and is preserved as a sauce. You can use bread dough for luting, if you wish, and it's quite pleasant to eat, but a firmer, less palatable 'luting paste' makes a surer seal.

Serves 6–12 as an appetizer

125g (1 cup) plain (all-purpose) flour (to seal the shells)
12 fresh scallops in shell
1 small shallot, very finely chopped
Small bunch of mixed sweet herbs

(parsley, tarragon, chives, thyme, chervil), finely chopped
Finely grated zest of ½ lemon
60g/¼ cup salted butter, softened
Drizzle of white vermouth
Freshly ground black pepper

Add water to the flour and work it between your fingers until it is the texture of quite tough clay. Roll it into a long sausage, about 1cm/½in thick, then flatten with your fingers into a thick ribbon.

Shuck the scallops and transfer them to a small bowl. Remove the black 'pipe' and trim the 'membrane' from the scallops, but leave the orange coral intact. Scrub and rinse the shells (if you have time, you can put them through the dishwasher).

Mix the shallot, herbs and lemon zest into the butter and season with black pepper. Put each scallop into the deep half of a shell with 1 tablespoon of the flavoured butter. Drizzle a little of the alcohol into each shell.

EGG SET UP
Direct set-up with the stainless steel grid or cast-iron grid on top.

TARGET TEMP
260°C/500°F

Cover each with the flat shell and seal the edges with the paste. Alternatively, seal the shells with foil if not using paste.

Burp and open the preheated EGG and cook for 3–5 minutes, with the dome closed, until the shells are bubbling and the scallops are lightly cooked. Don't overcook.

Serve on a platter and take directly to the table to unseal in front of your guests, using a safe, blunt knife to 'shuck' them. Be careful of the steam when you open them.

LONG SUMMER EVENINGS

There is a terrible downside to being organized and responsible about cooking for friends. Sometimes, when everything is rigorously planned and well lined up, you find that the evening moves quickly. Yes, sure, it's great for a restaurant kitchen to have you seated, served and the bill presented within two hours. They need to resell your table. But on a long summer's evening in your own back garden, it's a much better idea to stretch things out. This is one of my favourite menus, with a quick-to-table, physically interactive starter, a long slow-cook, substantial main and the sort of dessert you can pull out of the EGG, to applause and appreciation, later on and once the conversation is flowing.

SERVES 8–10

FEAST MENU

PORCHETTA: 2–4 hours cooking time 120–140°C/250–275°F

GRILLED ARTICHOKES WITH HOLLANDAISE: 1 hour cooking time 150–180°C/300–350°F

PATATAS 'BRAVAS': 1 hour 30 minutes cooking time 180–200°C/350–400°F

ELIZABETH DAVID'S SWAMP 'RAT': 30 minutes cooking time 180°C/350°F (220°C/425°F if on coals)

PINEAPPLE TATIN: 30 minutes cooking time 150–180°C/300–350°F

EGG FEAST SET UP
(if cooking everything together as a feast)

Load and light your EGG. Bring it to 140°C/275°F and add the convEGGtor basket with half moon baking stones bottom right and left, stainless steel grids top right and top left, a multi-level grid on top and a half moon cast-iron grid for later on in the cook.

FEAST METHOD
(if cooking everything together as a feast)

1 Cook the porchetta.

2 Cook the artichokes in the foil.

3 Cook the patatas on the multi-level grid; increase the temperature to 160–180°C/ 320–350°F to crackle the porchetta.

4 Remove the porchetta and the artichokes.

5 Remove the right half moon stainless steel grid and baking stone and replace with the half moon cast-iron searing grid; you may need to remove the patatas and the multi-level briefly to accommodate safely.

6 Once the half moon cast-iron grid has come to temperature, cook the bravas sauce and keep warm on the multi-level grid.

7 Cook the swamp rat.

8 Finish the artichoke on the half moon cast-iron grid.

9 Cook the pineapple tatin.

NOTE
Remember to burp your EGG when opening at high temperatures and cook with the dome closed.

PORCHETTA

Serves 6–8

1.5kg/3lb 5oz piece of pork middle, skin scored in 1cm/½in intervals

8 garlic cloves, sliced

2 tbsp rosemary leaves

2 tsp fennel seeds, toasted

1 tsp black peppercorns

1½ tsp salt

2 tbsp finely grated lemon zest

2 onions, roughly chopped (optional)

2 tbsp softened lard or olive oil

Porchetta is the tender, lean fillet of pork, wrapped in the flavourful fatty belly and great handfuls of garlic and Italian herbs. The long, slow, enclosed cooking in the EGG replicates a stone oven, giving all the juices and fats plenty of time to combine and distribute through the meat. It needs a good long rest after cooking – the Italians far prefer it warm, never hot. But if anything, it tastes even better a couple of days later, sliced cold with mayonnaise.

Lay the pork, skin-side down, on your chopping board. Remove all the bones.

Use a pestle and mortar or a spice grinder to smash the garlic, rosemary, fennel seeds, black peppercorns, salt and lemon zest together into a rough paste.

Smear the paste in a thick layer all over the meat, then roll it up tightly, starting on the loin side.

Tie the meat tightly at 3cm/1¼in intervals to form a cylinder of regular thickness.

Put the pork in a roasting rack in a drip tray with the onions and the lard or olive oil, burp and open the preheated EGG and roast to an internal temperature of 75°C/167°F, basting every 20 or so minutes. (The roasting tray catches any liquid so you can use it as a baste.) It just gets better the longer you can persuade it to cook. It can be fully cooked in 2 hours, but I'd be inclined to go for at least 4. Remember to always cook with the dome closed otherwise the temperature will soar.

Once the pork is cooked, burp and remove it from the EGG, then leave to rest for at least 30 minutes before slicing to serve.

EGG SET UP
Indirect set-up; the convEGGtor in the legs-up position with the stainless steel grid on top of the convEGGtor legs.

TARGET TEMP
120–140°C/250–275°F

GRILLED ARTICHOKES WITH HOLLANDAISE

Grilled artichokes with hollandaise are one of my all-time favourite summer foods. Grown up and sophisticated with an elegant hollandaise sauce, they are also romantic when shared and, for some reason, incredibly popular with small kids. You can do your hollandaise at the EGG, if you wish – the convEGGtor is terrific for controlling temperatures and delicate saucepan work – but, if you're still developing your confidence, you can make it up in advance and store it in a Thermos flask.

Serves 4–8

4 large globe artichokes

1 lemon, cut into 4 wedges

4 garlic cloves, left whole, but given a whack to slightly crush

1 large egg yolk

Juice of 1 lemon

200g/generous ¾ cup unsalted butter, melted

Olive oil, for brushing

Salt and freshly ground black pepper

EGG SET UP
Indirect set-up; the convEGGtor in the legs-up position with the stainless steel grid on top of the convEGGtor legs.

Then...
Direct set-up with the cast-iron grid.

TARGET TEMP
150–180°C/300–350°F

Wrap the artichokes individually in a double layer of foil, each with 2 tablespoons of water, a lemon wedge, a garlic clove and a big pinch of salt. Using the indirect set-up, burp and open your preheated EGG, place the wrapped artichokes on the stainless steel grid and leave them to steam for about 45–60 minutes with the dome closed until tender.

Meanwhile, for the hollandaise, put the egg yolk and 20ml/4 tsp of lemon juice into a heatproof bowl with 1 teaspoon of water and whisk together for 2–3 minutes until thick. Very

gradually, whisk in the melted butter (leaving the white milky solids behind) in a thin stream until thick and creamy. Season with salt, pepper and more lemon juice to taste. Keep the hollandaise sauce warm over a pan of boiling water off the heat, stirring occasionally.

Burp the EGG and remove the convEGGtor. Unwrap and halve the artichokes, top to bottom/ vertically, then paint the cut side with olive oil. Using the direct set-up, grid cut-side down on the bars in the EGG until golden brown. Sprinkle with salt to taste just before serving.

PATATAS 'BRAVAS'

Serves 4

2 red (bell) peppers

2 red chillies

2 dried ñora peppers (optional)

600g/1lb 5oz waxy potatoes, skin on, broken up into chunks

6 tbsp olive oil

1 onion, finely chopped

2 garlic cloves, finely chopped

2 tbsp sherry vinegar

1 x 400g/14oz can chopped tomatoes

2 tsp ground cumin

1 tsp smoked paprika, plus extra for dusting

1 tsp sweet paprika

Salt and freshly ground black pepper

I know. What are we thinking, combining Spanish potatoes with Italian pork? Maybe because they are both immeasurably enhanced by EGG cooking, because they go so well together, and ultimately, who's going to stop us? Remember to burp your EGG when opening at high temperatures and cook with the dome closed.

Roast the red peppers and fresh chillies directly on the grill in the preheated EGG for 20 minutes with the dome closed until softened and charred (or cook them directly in the coals to char more). Toast the ñora peppers (if using) on the grill for a minute or so, then remove the stems and seeds and rip into a few pieces. When the peppers and chillies are cooked, peel, remove the stems and seeds, roughly chop and place in a large, heatproof bowl with the ñora peppers.

Toss the potato chunks with 3 tablespoons of the olive oil and plenty of salt and pepper, arrange them in a single layer in a roasting tray or large skillet, then bake in the EGG for about 40 minutes with the dome closed until cooked and the edges are crispy.

Fry the onion and garlic in the remaining olive oil in a large pan for 10 minutes with the dome closed to soften. Add the vinegar and cook until it evaporates, then add the tomatoes, ground spices and a big pinch of salt, and simmer for about 15 minutes until thick and rich, stirring occasionally. Tip into the bowl with the peppers and chillies, then blend until smooth using a stick blender. Adjust the seasoning.

Spoon the bravas tomato sauce over the potatoes and toss to combine before serving.

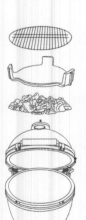

EGG SET UP
Indirect set-up; the convEGGtor in the legs-up position with the stainless steel grid on top of the convEGGtor legs.

TARGET TEMP
180–200°C/350–400°F

ELIZABETH DAVID'S SWAMP 'RAT'

I apologize for this, profoundly. Elizabeth David was the Goddess of British food writing, who led us into the glorious sunlight of Mediterranean cooking. She introduced my parents' generation to olive oil, garlic and fresh herbs, and her ratatouille and tians graced the tables of my childhood... which is why I'm childishly delighted by this redneck version. It's all the same ingredients and flavour but a little more vigorously combined and just a touch more BBQ than Dinner Party. Elizabeth might have disapproved, but you could consider slipping in a few slices of mozzarella alongside the veg.

Serves 4

4 large aubergines (eggplants)

2 onions, thinly sliced

4 courgettes (zucchini), sliced

2 red (bell) peppers, deseeded and cut into strips

4 large tomatoes, sliced

4 garlic cloves, thinly sliced

Generous amount of olive oil

Small bunch of basil or oregano, leaves picked

Salt and freshly ground black pepper

Make four long cuts along the length of each aubergine. Don't cut all the way through or to the ends. This should give you four 'pockets' in each aubergine.

Toss all the remaining vegetables and garlic individually in 2 tablespoons of olive oil (per vegetable), then season with salt and pepper. Add the basil or oregano.

Slip the vegetables into the slots/pockets in the aubergines, almost like folding things into the pages of a book, and then wrap each aubergine in foil. Just before sealing each parcel, glug in more olive oil.

Burp and open your preheated EGG and place the parcels directly in the fire or on the grill in the EGG for 15–20 minutes, cook with the dome closed. Serve in the foil parcels or, if you prefer, remove them from the foil and put them back in the EGG for 5 minutes to brown the tops.

EGG SET UP
Direct set-up with the stainless steel grid, or cook dirty on the charcoal.

TARGET TEMP
180°C/350°F
(220°C/425°F if on coals)

PINEAPPLE TATIN

Serves 8–10

1 small ripe pineapple, peeled and cored

50g/¼ cup golden granulated sugar

40g/3 tbsp butter

2 tbsp brandy, Cointreau, Grand Marnier or rum

1 x 375g/13oz packet of ready-rolled puff pastry sheet

Tatins are the most brilliant desserts to serve from the EGG. They are basically an upside-down tart, using a fruit or even a vegetable, which is caramelized, and a base of pre-made puff pastry cooked over the top. Flip the tart out to serve. You can make tatins with tomatoes, onions, carrots, parsnips, traditional apples or, in this case, slices of fresh pineapple, from which the sugars will caramelize magnificently. This is a quick and easy crowd-pleaser, which, if necessary, you can even prep 'on demand' if there's a sudden and urgent requirement for pudding.

Cut the pineapple widthways/across into slices, each slice about 3cm/1¼in thick.

Put the sugar into a large skillet. Burp and open the preheated EGG and heat very gently until the sugar dissolves and turns brown. Add the butter and booze, then stir with a wooden spoon to combine. Add the pineapple slices to the skillet, cut-side down, in a decorative arrangement (you may need to halve a couple or so to fit them all in), and cook for about 5 minutes with the dome closed.

Unroll the puff pastry and cut out a round slightly larger than the skillet. Burp the EGG and remove the skillet, then place the pastry on top of the pineapple, tucking it down the sides inside the skillet, being careful of the caramel. Add back to the EGG and close the dome.

Bake for 20–25 minutes until the pastry is puffed up and golden. Burp, then remove from the EGG and leave to rest for 5 minutes, then carefully invert the tatin onto a serving plate, taking care with the hot caramel.

EGG SET UP
Indirect set-up; the convEGGtor in the legs-up position with the stainless steel grid on top of the convEGGtor legs.

Then...
Direct set-up with the stainless steel grid or cast-iron grid.

TARGET TEMP
150–180°C/300–350°F

JAPANESE DINNER

In recent years, our interest in Japanese food has begun to expand beyond sushi and ramen. It's a fascinating and varied cuisine, taking on enormous influences from other food cultures. The EGG itself is derived from the Korean domestic grill – which is very similar to charcoal-fuelled ovens found in traditional Japanese homes – so it's a particularly appropriate cooking tool. Intriguingly, the Japanese favour 'Bincho' charcoal, which burns with very intense heat but is almost totally smokeless, so most of the flavour that fire cooking adds is the 'cleaner' note of char rather than the bassy notes of smoke.

SERVES 8–10

FEAST MENU

IBERICO TATAKI: a few minutes cooking time 250°C/480°F

SWEETCORN RICE: 30 minutes cooking time 140–160°C/275–320°F

MUSHROOM ENVELOPES: 15 minutes cooking time 170–200°C/325–400°F

YAKITORI-STYLE FISH: 15–25 minutes cooking time 150–180°C/300–350°F

FILLET IN SOY BUTTER: 2–3 minutes on each side cooking time 250°C/480°F

YAMITSUKI CABBAGE

CARROT AND BURDOCK SALAD: a few minutes cooking time 170–200°C/325–400°F

GRATED DAIKON WITH PONZU

NOTE

Remember to burp your EGG when opening at high temperatures and cook with the dome closed.

EGG FEAST SET UP

(if cooking everything together as a feast)

Load and light your EGG. Bring it to 170°C/325°F, setting up to cook direct; you will need a convEGGtor basket, half moon plancha and a half moon cast-iron searing grid. When cooking the tataki and steak, you will need to increase the temperature to 250°C/480°F.

FEAST METHOD

(if cooking everything together as a feast)

THE DAY BEFORE

1   Cook the Iberico tataki, so bring the EGG up to 250°C/480°F.

ON THE DAY

1   Cook the sweetcorn rice.

2   Whilst the rice is on, make the cabbage and the grated daikon.

3   Halfway through cooking the sweetcorn rice, cook the mushroom envelopes and the carrot and budock salad.

4   Prepare the tataki.

5   Remove the sweetcorn dish and rest whilst keeping the mushroom parcels warm.

6   Cook the fish.

7   Increase the temperature and cook the steak.

IBERICO TATAKI

One of the great advantages of the EGG is the ability to create cooking conditions you will never get in a domestic kitchen and therefore experiment with unusual preparations. Tataki is a method of hot-searing the outside of a 'single muscle' protein. It's often used to prepare an effectively raw food in a way that makes it more accessible. Tuna tataki is popular in Japanese restaurants outside of Japan where people might baulk at sashimi; it's also a great way to present high-quality beef fillet. Here, though, we're going to use the extreme heat of the EGG to sear the outside of an Iberico pork fillet. It's a fantastic meat, taken from the free-ranging pigs reared to make Iberico ham in Extremadura in Spain. It's available from specialist mail order companies online, or your butcher may be able to find it for you. The cuts are small and deliciously marbled with fat, but the very high heat of the EGG enables you to sear even tiny pieces without damaging the meat within. A domestic frying pan would just cook the meat through before it browned.

Prepare the marinade by combining the soy sauce, mirin, rice wine vinegar and sesame oil in a freezeproof container. I'm not keen on sweet marinades, but if you are, consider whisking in a little honey to taste. Grate in 50g/1¾oz of the ginger. Put the marinade into the freezer so it gets very cold, though doesn't actually freeze, about 1 hour.

Carefully trim the pork loin or fillet of extraneous fat. This is delicate work and worth doing well. On smaller fillets, I've even used a scalpel before now.

If you can only get small fillets, use a plancha or cast-iron skillet on the EGG, preheated above 250°C/480°F. If you have larger fillets and you're confident and quick with your tongs, you can try it 'on-the-bars'. Sear as fast as you can. You should be looking at convincing browning within 20–30 seconds. When opening the EGG at high temperatures always remember to burp it. Keep the meat moving constantly until it's fully seared. Plunge the fillet straight into the chilled marinade, fully coat it, cover and refrigerate overnight.

While the meat is still very cold, dry it on paper towels, then slice, sashimi-style (thinly sliced or cut into bite-sized pieces), with a deadly sharp knife. Discard the marinade. Arrange on a plate and allow to rise to room temperature before serving with a dipping sauce made of dark soy sauce, rice wine vinegar, the rest of the grated ginger and a few drops of sesame oil.

Serves 4

200ml/7fl oz dark soy sauce
75ml/2½fl oz mirin
60ml/2fl oz rice wine vinegar
A few drops of sesame oil
Honey, to taste (optional)
75g/2½oz fresh ginger, peeled
500g/1lb 2oz loin or fillet of Iberico pork

EGG SET UP
Direct set-up with the stainless steel grid or cast-iron grid on top.

TARGET TEMP
250°C/480°F

SWEETCORN RICE

It's little short of magical how well the buttery flavours and sweetness of the corn enhance the rice, but it's also pretty amazing how well it goes with almost any barbecued food. Maybe it just has all the right flavour notes to fit our expectations of outdoor eating. The really cool thing, though, is that cooking rice on the EGG, actually makes a better job of it than having someone else knock it up in the kitchen while you grill. The Japanese donabe-style pot is designed to be used on live fire and uses it's own recycled steam so the rice is extra-fluffy. Sweetcorn rice will transform all your feasts, so don't save it for Japanese meals, spread the love. You can use a cast-iron or earthenware casserole, but put a sheet of foil over the top before closing the lid to improve the seal. The Japanese cook rice by volume. The Goh is the standard volume for a single portion, around 180ml.

Rinse the Japanese rice until the water runs clear. Put the rice into the bottom of your donabe, then break up half the butter and dot it over the top.

Strip the corn kernels off the cobs using a large, sharp knife, then layer the kernels over the top of the rice. Lay the stripped cobs on top of that – they still have flavour to add.

Add the sake to your measure, top up with water and pour into the pot, followed by three more goh measures of water. Put the lid on, burp and open the preheated EGG and place on the bars. After 10–15 minutes of cooking with the dome closed, open the dome and you'll start to see a little steam leaking from the pot or hear bubbling; at which point, move it to the coolest place on your bars without lifting the lid, and close the dome. This is the magical part. The pot, just like the body of your EGG, is now holding heat and, with very little extra input, will keep gently steaming and simmering for another 15 minutes or so, by which point most of the liquid and flavours will have been absorbed by the rice. Burp your EGG and move the pot off the heat but still don't remove the lid of the pot.

Because ceramic retains heat, the pot will continue to steam the rice until the last of the moisture is absorbed, but it won't burn because you're no longer adding 'extra' heat. The donabe will keep rice warm throughout the meal, but it will be at its peak after a 15-minute 'rest' off the heat.

After resting, lift the lid, remove the cobs, season the rice with the soy sauce and glaze with the last of the butter, then mix everything together and fluff with a fork.

Serves 6–8

3 goh Nishiki rice (540g/19oz)
15g/1 tbsp butter
2 corn on the cob, husks and silks removed
2 tsp sake
10g/¼oz dark soy sauce

EGG SET UP
Direct set-up with the stainless steel grid or cast-iron grid.

TARGET TEMP
140–160°C/
275–320°F

MUSHROOM ENVELOPES – HOIRU YAKI

Hoiru yaki means 'foil cooking' in Japanese. It's a useful technique in a country where most homes don't have large domestic ovens like ours but favour instead bench-top fan ovens. The foil encloses the food with liquid and aromatics and enables contained steaming – not unlike the more classic French 'en papillotte' method. Mushrooms respond particularly well to this style of cooking, yielding a fantastically rich and concentrated juice in which they effectively self-stew.

Serves 4

500g/1lb 2oz fresh Japanese mushrooms (enoki, eryngii/king oyster, maitake, shimeji, shiitake)

4 spring onions (scallions)

1 red or green chilli

8g/¼oz fresh ginger, peeled

2 garlic cloves, peeled

40ml/1¼fl oz dark soy sauce

40ml/1¼fl oz Japanese beer

40ml/1¼fl oz mirin

80g/6 tbsp butter

Fold a length of foil in half, then fold a seam up two sides to create an open-topped foil bag. Put your hand inside and push down onto a flat surface so the bag stands up. Make one of these for each diner.

Pick through your mushrooms, removing any dirt and trimming off any dried-out areas. I like to tear the bigger mushrooms into more manageable chunks, and the enoki will probably

EGG SET UP
Direct set-up; the convEGGtor basket with the half moon, or stainless steel grid and baking stone.

TARGET TEMP
170–200°C/325–400°F

need to be split apart a little. Distribute the mushrooms amongst your foil bags.

Shred the spring onions, slice the chilli and cut the ginger into matchsticks before distributing them evenly between the bags. Add a grating of garlic to each.

Distribute the liquids evenly between the bags – a big glug each of the soy sauce, beer and mirin – then drop a big knob of butter into each. Roll down the top of each bag and pinch to seal. Be sure to allow enough space for the steam to circulate.

Burp and open the preheated EGG and place the foil bags in the EGG and close the dome. Check one bag after 15 minutes to see if the mushrooms are cooked through. The mushrooms will continue to cook gently in the bags until they're unsealed.

YAKITORI-STYLE WHOLE FISH

Serves 6–8

1 whole turbot, sea bass, brill or sea bream, about 1.5kg/3lb 5oz, gutted, trimmed and cleaned

Neutral oil, for brushing

Flaky sea salt

100ml/3½fl oz tare (see page 247)

There is an excellent technique for grilling whole fish that's popular in Galicia. They use a fish 'cage' or a double-sided enclosing grill so the fish can be rotated then start searing over quite a high heat on one side. As the fish begins to sear, they flip it over and 'cool' the cooked side with a mixture of salty brine, lemon juice, oil and flavouring herbs. This slows the cooking process while the other side is also beginning to sear, then it's flipped over and sprayed down with the magic liquid. This process is repeated many times. Like spit cooking, oils and fats don't escape from the fish because the constant flipping means they flow back towards the centre. The liquid builds up a salty crust and the cooking process is slowed so flavours can permeate.

This is so close to the techniques of yakitori, and the Tare on chicken is so suitable a match for fish, that it seems daft not to try the technique on whole fish if you can get your hands on a fish cage. Use the Tare recipe (see page 247) and a clean plastic spray bottle to apply it, which gives a much better result than trying to brush it on.

In the picture, we're giving the yakitori treatment to a nice little sea bream, but a Galician would prefer a larger turbot, which is quite wise if you're scaling up. A turbot is a lot more fish in a flatter format.

Dry the skin of the prepared fish, brush with oil, season with salt and place in a fish grilling cage. Make the tare.

Place the fish in its cage on the grill in the preheated EGG, cook for 5 minutes on each side, then brush or spray with the tare. Continue to cook and turn every 3–5 minutes, brushing or spraying with the tare as you go. Cook until you have an internal temperature of 55°C/131°F or more in the thickest part of the fish.

Gently remove the fish from the cage and either take it off the bone by cutting down the backbone and gently lifting off the fillets, or leave it whole to serve.

EGG SET UP
Direct set-up with the stainless steel grid or cast-iron grid on top.

TARGET TEMP
150–180°C/300–350°F

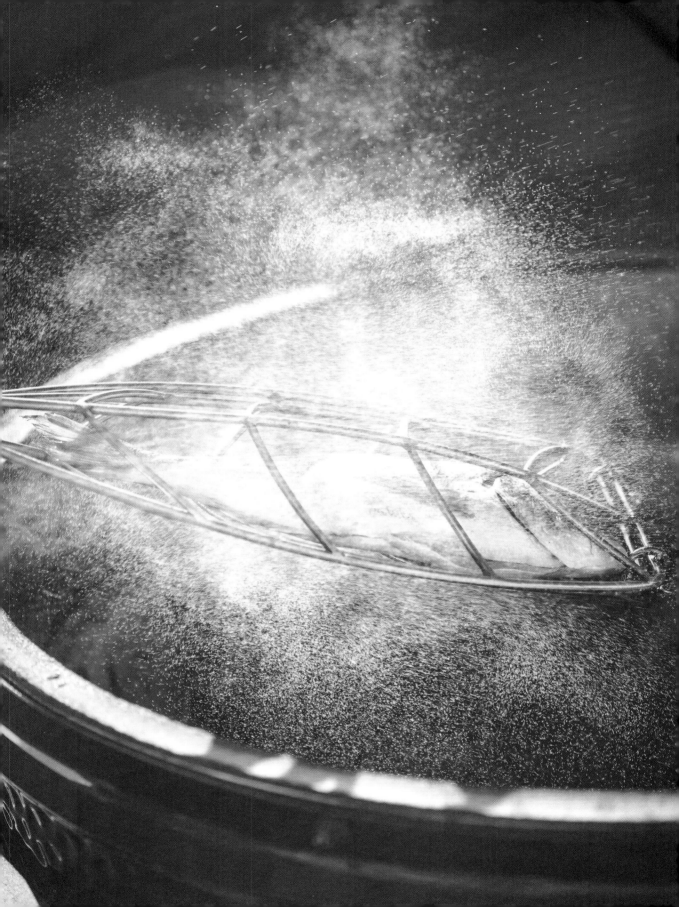

FILLET IN SOY BUTTER

Serves 4 as an appetizer/part of the feast or 1 person as a main course

1 fillet steak approx. 300g/10½oz
20g/1½ tbsp butter
4 tsp dark soy sauce
Ground black pepper

It's funny how quickly food ideas spread across the world now we've got the internet to help us. Throughout culinary history, we've had no concept of umami or fermented soy ingredients in the West, while in Japan there was almost no history of dairy use in cooking, particularly of butter. Historically, the Japanese considered that it was the consumption of butter that made Europeans smell so distinctive. They called us bata-kusai or 'butterstinkers'.

Now, quite suddenly, all over the world, the spectacular union of soy and butter is being discovered by chefs and cooks. Just when you thought there was nothing as good as melted butter, you discover that soy doubles its gloriousness. Just when you thought that nothing could enhance soy's ability to increase flavour, you realize that melted butter enables it to coat the tongue and trigger receptors. Soy brings umami, butter brings 'mouthfeel' and it's a match made in heaven.

And what's the best way to use soy butter? A very classic French technique of butter basting called 'arroser'. The literal translation is 'sprinkling' but I prefer the more spiritual overtones of 'anointing'. Here's how it's done with a simple steak, but you can do this with any piece of meat, poultry or fish and your tongue will thank you.

Open and burp your preheated EGG and grill the meat on the bars over a high heat. You want a decent char on the outside, but pull it off when it gets to 30°C/90°F on your probe thermometer.

Transfer the meat into a frying pan. You'll need one with plenty of space and curved sides. You'll also need a spoon that complements this curve. This is a very personal thing that may take a while to finesse. (I should also warn you that it might result in you coming across the correct spoon in the possession of someone else – a friend or relative perhaps – and subsequently having to trouser it. Once you have your pan and spoon to your liking, you are sorted for life.) Add a large knob of the butter to the pan and put it back onto the bars.

Take the pan handle in your non-dominant hand and lift it so the pan is at an angle and the butter begins to pool at the

EGG SET UP
Direct set-up with the stainless steel grid or cast-iron grid on top.

TARGET TEMP
250°C/480°F

continued overleaf...

edge. Pour half the soy sauce over the steak, then begin spooning the butter up and over the meat. It will run off and pool again at the side of the pan, but keep spooning.

After a few seconds, flip the steak, pour over the remaining soy sauce and start basting again.

You can flip again, if you wish, and add more butter, if health advice is not your thing, but bear in mind that the plan is to lift the steak when it still has a glistening coating of butterfat adhering to its surface, which will get even more gloriously co-mingled with the crispy seared crust of the meat as it rests. Which it will, of course, for at least 10 minutes, but preferably longer. Slice thickly to serve.

YAMITSUKI CABBAGE

This is the cabbage supplied on bar tops all over Japan to enhance the enjoyment of beer and quite possibly to promote increased consumption. Like many bar snacks, it relies on salt to work its magic, but in this case, it also makes a very felicitous balance between the sweet flavour of raw cabbage and the nuttiness of sesame.

Some recipes recommend the use of a large pinch of chicken stock powder in the dressing, which actually tastes pretty good, but when Western writers mention stock powder, they're usually trying to avoid mentioning MSG, which is a much more effective flavour enhancer. I'm happy to say you can forget chicken stock, because this dish is spectacular with a light sprinkle of Aji-no-moto, the crystalline MSG commonly used for seasoning in Japan. There is, however, a brilliant source of umami in British cooking, which is mustard powder. Not the made stuff, the powder. It also, tangentially, has a flavour resonance with the slightly sulphurous tang of the cabbage. English mustard powder is a horrible corruption of the original recipe, but it's even more sensational.

Cut the cabbage into large square chunks and place in a bowl. Add the salt and massage it hard into the cabbage. Encourage the salt flakes to scratch up the surface of the leaves.

Mix together the mustard powder, garlic and sesame oil, then pour over the cabbage and mix thoroughly. Toast the sesame seeds in a dry pan and sprinkle over the cabbage.

Serves 4 as a side

½ head of white cabbage (though choose one with plenty of green in it)

10g/¼oz coarse salt flakes

Pinch of English mustard powder

¼ garlic clove, crushed

4 tsp sesame oil

10g/¼oz sesame seeds

CARROT AND BURDOCK SALAD

Serves 4–6

500g/1lb 2oz fresh burdock root

250g/9oz carrots, peeled

20ml/1 tbsp sesame oil

20ml/1 tbsp soy sauce

20ml/1 tbsp mirin

10g/1 tbsp sesame seeds

5g/1 tbsp chilli flakes (red pepper flakes), optional

This is the simplest possible stir-fry-and-braise. Carrot and burdock go so well together and can be served hot or as a cold salad, so it's worth getting the wok out and doing a reasonable-sized batch. Burdock root is available through Chinese, Japanese and Korean specialist stores. Many of them also sell burdock chopped and frozen or pre-braised in plastic pouches... a really great larder standby. This also works surprisingly well with parsnips... though you need to cut back on the mirin if you don't like it too sweet.

Scrub the burdock root but leave the skin on. Cut into 5cm/2in lengths and then julienne strips. Soak in a bowl of cold water for 30 minutes, then drain. Julienne the carrots to the same size.

Burp and open your preheated EGG and add your wok. Add the burdock root to the hot wok and stir-fry. Do this dry, initially, to drive off the soaking water, then add half the sesame oil.

When the burdock begins to soften, add the carrots, then the rest of the sesame oil. After about 30 seconds of stir-frying, add the soy sauce and mirin.

Keep stirring as the liquid cooks away. You're cooking the veg in a highly aromatic steam, which will reduce to a fabulous sweet/salty glaze.

As soon as the vegetables are tender, dry and shiny, pour them into a bowl and dress with the sesame seeds, and chilli flakes if you fancy. Serve hot or serve cold as a salad.

EGG SET UP
Direct set-up with the stainless steel grid, plus the Big Green Egg wok. Or even the convEGGtor basket with the wok.

TARGET TEMP
170–200°C/325–400°F

GRATED DAIKON WITH PONZU

This might just be the simplest side dish known to man, yet it's somehow enormously greater than the sum of its parts. Ponzu shoyū is a pretty amazing dressing, and the turnip/radish flavour of the daikon is very different to most of our preconceptions of 'salad' and complements it spectacularly. You can buy ponzu shoyū ready-made in Japanese grocers, but it's a lovely thing to make from scratch and it's one of those things you'll want to develop your own personal recipe for. Take this as a starting point. Ponzu will keep in the fridge for a couple of weeks in a stoppered bottle, though I usually find any left over is demanded by friends to take away.

Ponzu is a citrus sauce, traditionally made with yuzu, which is difficult to find outside of Japan. Yuzu's flavour is usually defined as 'somewhere between grapefruit and orange/lemon/lime/satsuma', which is rather convenient because replicating it with those fruits gives us all sorts of variations we can make to our own preferences. I start with the juice of a whole grapefruit and half a lime and then take it from there, depending on what's available. It's entirely down to your own taste but, unless you're using orange and/or satsuma, you might find you need a little sugar in the mix.

Ponzu starts with a dashi. Warm the mirin and rice vinegar in a small saucepan on the hob and then add the kombu and katsuobushi and allow to infuse on the heat for a few minutes, then remove from the heat. This isn't a matter of simmering. It's far better to just keep everything warm and let the flavours combine gently. The seaweed adds umami and the dried bonito flakes bring a smokiness. Tune these flavours to your own taste by varying the amount of time each infuses for. Strain the cooled dashi into a bowl.

Mix your choice of citrus juices up to 150ml/5fl oz and add to the dashi. Add sugar to taste, if you like, then stir in the soy sauce. There's space for infinite tweaking here, but remember that the basic core of the sauce is equal parts of soy, citrus and dashi.

The final ingredient is rice vinegar to bring everything into balance. The amount you use will vary, depending on how sour your citrus component is, so keep tasting as you mix it in.

Meanwhile, peel your daikon and grate it into a colander. Let it drain for an hour or two, then heap it into small serving bowls and pour over the ponzu.

Serves 4–6

150ml/5fl oz mirin

100ml/3½fl oz rice wine vinegar, plus extra to taste

1 piece of kombu (seaweed)

15g/½oz katsuobushi (dried bonito flakes)

Juice of 1 grapefruit

Juice of limes, lemons, oranges, satsumas (see method)

Sugar, to taste (optional)

150ml/5fl oz light soy sauce

1 daikon radish

TACO PARTY

We tend to look to the USA as the homeland of BBQ and grilling, but for me, things start to get really exciting when you cross the border and head south. Let's just admit, straight from the outset, that it would be daft to try to bring together all the insanely diverse cuisines of Central and South America in any meaningful way. But it is possible to cherry-pick a couple of very exciting ones. In Argentina, a parrilla can mean a grill for cooking, a restaurant specializing in grilled meats, or a kind of all-day family picnic out in the countryside, centred around a fire and grill. It would be good to bring a little of all of that spirit to a feast. Our second influence is the cuisine of Mexico – still strangely unexplored by food lovers in Europe but surely one of the most exciting and varied in the world.

SERVES 10–14

FEAST MENU

SALSA CHIMICHURRI: 20-30 minutes cooking time 140°C/275°F

SALSA VERDE: 20-30 minutes cooking time 140°C/275°F

CHARRED SALSA: 10–15 minutes cooking time 140°C/275°F

TACO AL PASTOR: 2½–3½ hours cooking time 120–140°C/250–275°F

MATAMBRE ARROLLADO: 1½–2 hours cooking time 160–180°C/320–350°F

RAJAS DE POBLANO: 20–30 minutes cooking time 180°C/350°F

FISH TACOS : 3–5 minutes cooking time 180°C/350°F

FLOUR TORTILLAS: 1½ minutes cooking time for each 190–210°C/375–410°F

EGG FEAST SET UP
(if cooking everything together as a feast)

Load and light your EGG. Bring it to 140°C/275°F, add two half moon baking stones to the lower level of the convEGGtor basket, and two half moon stainless steel grids on the level above. You will later need to also remove one half moon baking stone and stainless steel grid and replace it with a half moon plancha and a multi level grid on top of the convEGGtor basket.

continued overleaf...

continued overleaf...

FEAST METHOD

(if cooking everything together as a feast)

THE DAY BEFORE

1   Make up the marinade for your taco al pastor. Once cool, pour two-thirds over the meat and leave in the fridge for 8 hours or overnight.

2   Make all your sauces first so they are out of the way and you won't have to worry about them later. Start with the salsa verde, which benefits from resting before serving, and the chimichurri, which should be cooked at 140°C/275°F on the baking stone side (indirect).

3   Make the charred salsa, charring the vegetables on the cast-iron searing grid side (direct).

4   Beat out the matambre, then paint the inner surface with the chimichurri and leave in the fridge for up to 8 hours.

5   Make the tortillas, if you wish or on the day.

ON THE DAY

1   Remove the half moon cast-iron searing grid and replace with the second half moon baking stone. Add the two stainless steel grids on top. The grill is now fully indirect at 140°C/275°F.

2   Stack the meat onto the skewers for the al pastor, then place the assembled pile into the EGG.

3   Build the matambre.

4   After an hour, add the matambre to the EGG.

5   Once cooked, remove the meat from the EGG.

6   Turn the temperature up to 180°C/350°F, remove one of the baking stones and stainless steel grids and replace with a half moon plancha.

7   Make the rajas de poblano on the baking stone side (indirect) and the fish taco filling on the plancha side (direct).

8   To reheat all the elements of your feast, add the multi-level rack.

9   Heat the tortillas.

NOTES

1   Have all your ingredients prepared, for all the recipes, before you start to cook the al pastor.

2   If you're cooking the rajas de poblano at the same time, use the convEGGtor inside the EGGspander to move the al pastor out of the way. Alternatively, you could cook the rajas de poblano amongst the coals at the same time as the garlic for the salsa verde and the charred salsa.

3   Remember to burp your EGG when opening at high temperatures and cook with the dome closed.

4   Cook the fish tacos, and warm through the tortillas and rajas de poblano, while the taco al pastor rests.

5   Serve with lime wedges, finger bowls and napkins.

SALSA CHIMICHURRI

Chimichurri has a lot in common with a classic French salad dressing... but it's far less uptight. There's a lot of chopped herbage in there, including some very assertive oregano, plus enough chilli to perk you right up and, once again, we're going to roast the garlic for sweetness. But this stuff is insanely versatile. It goes with meat, fish and poultry. Dip your tortillas straight in it, use it as a marinade or pour it on as you grill. Here we're making it just so we can paint it inside the matambre... but always make way too much. You'll never run out of ways to use it.

Wrap the whole garlic head in a sheet of foil brushed with olive oil. Burp and open your preheated EGG and roast the garlic for about 20–30 minutes, with the dome closed, until soft and sweet, then squeeze the flesh out of the papery skin and leave to cool. Blend the garlicky paste together with everything else in a bowl until smooth, adding salt and pepper to taste, and more vinegar to balance, plus more oil if necessary to manage the consistency.

Makes about 250g/9oz

1 head of garlic

1 tsp dried oregano, or 8 tbsp chopped fresh oregano

2 tbsp vinegar

Juice of ½ lemon

½ tsp chilli flakes (red pepper flakes)

Small bunch of parsley, chopped

1 shallot, finely chopped

70ml/5 tbsp olive oil, plus extra for brushing

Salt and freshly ground black pepper

EGG SET UP
Indirect set-up; the convEGGtor in the legs-up position with the stainless steel grid on top of the convEGGtor legs.

TARGET TEMP
140°C/275°F

SALSA VERDE

Salsa verde is one of the freshest and brightest of the South American salsas, featuring fresh herbs and chillies on a base of tomatillo, which is a larger and far more interesting relative of the physalis. If you're lucky, you might find fresh tomatillos, but they are brilliant in cans too – search online.

Wrap the whole head of garlic in a sheet of foil brushed with olive oil, burp and open your preheated EGG and roast the garlic for about 20–30 minutes, with the dome closed, until softened. Squeeze the flesh out of the scorched skin and leave to cool. This will add smokiness and slightly sweeten the garlic. Not traditional but nonetheless delicious.

Blend the garlicky paste together with everything else in a bowl until smooth, tasting as you go, and correcting with salt and more lime. Cover and refrigerate until ready to serve.

Makes about 250g/9oz

1 head of garlic

Olive oil, for brushing

4 jalapeño chillies, stems removed and finely chopped

Juice of 1 lime, plus more to taste

1 small bunch of coriander (cilantro), coarsely chopped

2 tomatillos, finely chopped

Salt

EGG SET UP
Indirect set-up; the convEGGtor in the legs-up position with the stainless steel grid on top of the convEGGtor legs.

TARGET TEMP
140°C/275°F

CHARRED SALSA

It's funny how much people worry about 'burning' things when cooking over charcoal. Particularly over the last few years, even the poshest chefs have caught up with the idea that the proper scorching – actual carbonization – is a whole separate set of tools for flavour. Scorched skin on (bell) peppers and capsicums balances their heat and sweetness. Onions and garlic can have their papery outer skins burned entirely black and, when they're peeled later, they've just enhanced the flesh inside with subtle smoke. This is a fairly standard South American salsa made glorious by savage heating.

Burp then open your preheated EGG and grill the whole tomatoes, red pepper, spring onions and garlic for about 10–15 minutes, turning every now and then until blistered and charred, when not turning, cook with the dome closed. Remove from the EGG. Remove the skins from the tomatoes, pepper and garlic, and deseed the pepper. Don't worry about leaving some charred bits on there, as they really boost the flavour.

Either finely chop or use a pestle and mortar to give a coarse texture to the charred vegetables. Avoid blending until smooth. Season liberally with salt and pepper, then add the coriander and lime juice, and add chilli to adjust to your own heat levels.

Cover and refrigerate until needed.

Serves 8–14

400g/14oz ripe tomatoes

1 red (bell) pepper

Bunch of spring onions (scallions), trimmed

4 garlic cloves, unpeeled

Small bunch of coriander (cilantro), finely chopped

Juice of 1 lime

1–3 tsp Arbol chilli flakes, or another medium/hot fresh chilli (finely chopped), according to your tolerance

Salt and freshly ground black pepper

EGG SET UP
Direct set-up with the stainless steel grid or cast-iron grid on top.

TARGET TEMP
140°C/275°F

RAJAS DE POBLANO

Serves 6–8 as a side

6 poblano peppers, or use 3 green (bell) peppers and a couple of mild green chillies

1 onion

4 garlic cloves, peeled and left whole

300g/10½oz soured (sour) cream or crème fraîche

200g/7oz Oaxaca or low-moisture mozzarella cheese, grated

Salt and freshly ground black pepper

Both peppers and onions have a high moisture content. When they're grilled over a high heat, they char, adding complexity, and they give off moisture that's also full of light vegetal flavour notes. This technique works well with fruity flavoured peppers like poblanos but also with more common red or green (bell) peppers. You can treat this like a dip, scooping it up with tortilla chips, or as a side vegetable.

Wrap the peppers (and chillies, if using), onion and garlic in a double layer of foil with a big pinch of salt. Burp and open your preheated EGG, then place the vegetables directly in the hot coals for 20–30 minutes, with the dome closed, until softened and a bit charred. Once you've checked they're cooked, reseal the foil and let them rest and steam. Keep the foil parcel in a bowl so you don't lose any of the precious liquid.

Pick as much charred skin as possible from the peppers (and chillies), removing the stems and ribs. You can control the heat of the finished dish by how many seeds you leave in.

Slice the peppers into strips, the onion into thin slices and smash the garlic with the side of your knife, then add to a pan with the soured cream, seasoning with salt and a generous amount of black pepper. Pour in any extra liquid you managed to catch in the foil or the bowl, then gently reheat the mixture and stir in the cheese until it's fully melted.

EGG SET UP
Direct set-up; cook directly on the charcoal.

If cooking for the feast, cook directly on the charcoal under the al pastor, that is cooking indirectly.

TARGET TEMP
180°C/350°F

TACO AL PASTOR

Taco 'al pastor', or shepherd-style, was introduced to Mexico by Lebanese immigrants. It's derived from the vertical spit cooking we're used to in kebab grilling, but using highly marinated pork instead of lamb. This method uses small skewers to create a mini 'doner' which fits beautifully into an EGG. The juices can be basted back over the meat and, once servings have been sliced off the outside, the whole thing can be put back into the heat for a second round of crisp browning.

Serves 10–14

1 pork belly, boned and sliced into 1cm/½in thick pieces, roughly 15cm/6in across

1 pork shoulder, boned and sliced into 1cm/½in thick pieces, roughly 15cm/6in across

1 smallish pineapple, cut in half horizontally (keep the stalk on for visual effect, if you prefer)

For the marinade/baste
2 ancho chillies
2 pasilla chillies
6 garlic cloves, peeled
3 tbsp vegetable oil
1 tsp annatto seeds
1 tsp Mexican dried oregano
1 tsp salt
1 tsp ground cinnamon
2 tsp ground cumin
¼ tsp ground cloves
2–3 tsp chipotle chilli flakes (red pepper flakes)
½ tsp cracked black pepper
Juice of 1 orange

EGG SET UP
Indirect set-up; the convEGGtor in the legs-up position with the stainless steel grid on top of the convEGGtor legs.

TARGET TEMP
120–140°C/250–275°F

TO MAKE THE MARINADE

Remove the stems and seeds from the chillies, burp and open your preheated EGG and then toast the chillies in a pan with the garlic cloves for 1 minute. Remove the pan, closing the dome, and then tip the chillies into a bowl (set the garlic aside), cover with freshly boiled water from the kettle and leave to soak.

Heat the vegetable oil in the same pan on the EGG and fry the annatto seeds for 30 seconds or until the oil is a deep red colour. Strain the oil (discarding the seeds), then leave to one side.

continued overleaf...

Blend the garlic with the soaked chillies, 100ml/scant ½ cup of the soaking liquid, the oregano, salt, ground spices, chilli flakes and black pepper to make a smooth sauce.

Burp and open the EGG and fry the blended sauce in the annatto oil for 5 minutes, with the dome closed, or until most of the liquid has evaporated and the sauce is beginning to brown and stick to the bottom of the pan. Stir in the orange juice and add salt to taste. Leave to cool. Use two-thirds of the mix to marinate the meat for at least 2 hours.

TO PREPARE AND COOK

You'll need a large metal skewer with no 'head' or 'handle' and three 15cm/6in metal skewers.

Start with the large skewer, stood vertically on your chopping board, point upwards. Place your smallest piece of marinated meat on the skewer and push it to the bottom.

Add the rest of the meat, alternating belly and shoulder, with each layer getting generally bigger.

Once all the meat is loaded up you should be looking at something like an inverted meaty Christmas tree. Use the three 15cm/6in skewers to nail the meat together by inserting them diagonally through the meat stack, to create a kind of tripod arrangement.

Withdraw the large guide skewer and flip the meaty tower onto its three 'feet' in a cast-iron skillet or baking dish. Where the three points appear at the top of your porky pyramid, jam on the top half of the pineapple like a jaunty hat. Squeeze the meat tightly together and wrap tightly in foil. Allow to rest in the fridge for 2–8 hours.

Remove the foil, burp and open the EGG and cook the meat for about 1½–2 hours in the skillet/dish, ideally sat up, but otherwise on its side turning halfway through if required. Keep the dome closed whilst cooking.

Burp and open the EGG and spoon the remaining marinade over the meat, double wrap in foil and then cook for another 1–1½ hours, with the dome closed, until the internal temperature is 93–95°C/199–203°F. Open the EGG, remove the foil for the last 30 minutes, to promote browning and to allow basting with the juices in the pan. Keep the dome closed when not basting.

Remove from the EGG and leave to rest for 30 minutes before slicing into shreds and serving with the cooking juices. Leave the top of the pineapple in place but squeeze it over the meat. Peel, core and thickly slice the leftover bottom part of the pineapple, then sear it quickly on the grill bars.

Serve in tortillas with the grilled pineapple slices and salsas.

MATAMBRE ARROLLADO

Serves 4–6

1 skirt or flank steak

4 tbsp salsa chimichurri (see page 149), plus extra to serve

2 tbsp olive oil

1 large onion, finely chopped

4 garlic cloves, grated

1 red (bell) pepper, deseeded and cut into strips

2 green (bell) peppers, deseeded and cut into strips

2 carrots, coarsely grated

Bunch of flat-leaf parsley, finely chopped

6 hard-boiled eggs, cooled and peeled

Salt and freshly ground black pepper

Butcher's string

Matambre Arrollado translates, rather pleasingly, as 'Rolled Hunger-killer'. Probably best to use the original Spanish on the menu though. It's a cheap but very flavourful cut of meat, beaten out thin then wrapped around cheap ingredients and flavourings. I usually make a couple of these at a time because a) it's so good cold the next day, in a roll with chimichurri and mayo, and b) nobody ever leaves any when it's served hot.

Lay the steak on the chopping board so the grain of the meat is running straight ahead of you. Slice down the centre line, halfway through the meat. Now very carefully slice outwards, left and right towards the edges. Take your time and use a very sharp knife. Stop before you reach the edges and you should eventually be able to open out two flaps on either side so the whole steak is now twice as wide as it was and half as thick.

Place the steak between two pieces of butcher's paper (or baking paper) and beat it out even thinner.

Only kidding. Get your butcher to do all of this, if you prefer.

Season the meat with salt and pepper. Apply a layer of salsa chimichurri to the top side and put it in the fridge for anything up to 8 hours.

Burp and open your preheated EGG, heat the olive oil in a cast-iron pan and soften the onion, garlic and peppers for 10 minutes with the dome closed, adding ½ teaspoon of salt, then allow to cool.

Lay the meat out on a sheet of cling film (plastic wrap) and cover with a thick layer of the grated carrots, then the softened vegetables and the parsley.

Cut two eggs in half and lay the halves in a line in the centre of the meat, along the grain. Lay the remaining four whole eggs in a line up the left-hand edge of the steak. Season with more pepper.

Roll the meat around the whole eggs first, then keep going, using the cling film to lift and control the meat as you continue, incorporating the half eggs and all the filling. Tie with butcher's string at 5cm/2in intervals to secure. Then wrap the entire thing first in cling film and then in foil.

Burp the EGG and roast for about 1–1½ hours with the dome closed until tender, unwrapping for the last 20 minutes, so the outside surface can colour and crisp a little.

Serve hot in thick slices, or cold and thinly sliced, with extra salsa chimichurri and loads of mayo.

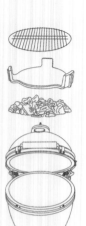

EGG SET UP
Indirect set-up; the convEGGtor in the legs-up position with the stainless steel grid on top of the convEGGtor legs.

TARGET TEMP
160–180°C/
320–350°F

FISH TACOS

Serves 6

6 firm white fish fillets
Salt

For the rub
Grated zest and juice of 1 small orange (you can use a Seville orange in season)

Grated zest and juice of ½ lime

2 garlic cloves, crushed

2 tsp chipotle chilli powder (or use 1 tbsp chipotle in adobo)

1 tsp ground cumin

1 tsp soft brown sugar

½ tsp salt

½ tsp freshly ground black pepper

3 tbsp olive or vegetable oil

To serve
Tortillas/tacos

3 ripe avocados, peeled, stoned and thinly sliced

Nothing beats a fish taco on a hot day, but traditional recipes favour pieces of fish that are battered and deep-fried. I yield to no man in my love of deep-fried things but they can be too filling. Personally, I prefer to grill a large piece of white fish, suitably marinated, so it has a delicious crust but flakes easily. Apart from the fact that these taste infinitely better, there seems to be no limit to how many you can eat.

Salt the fish the night before you intend to use it and refrigerate overnight. This seasons the fish but also firms it up a little.

Pat the fillets dry with paper towels. Mix all the rub ingredients together, then apply comprehensively to the fish.

Burp and open your preheated EGG and place the fillets on the grid or plancha for about 3–5 minutes until the flesh is just cooked through and flakes when you pull it apart (cooking time depends on the thickness of the fish and heat of the grill).

If your fish has skin, you can place it straight onto a hot plancha or skillet, then close the dome so the skin crisps and the flesh just cooks through from the reflected heat of the dome. By not flipping the fish, even more juiciness is retained.

Burp your EGG, remove the fish and let it rest for maybe 30 seconds, then flake into tortillas or tacos with sliced avocado and salsas.

EGG SET UP
Direct set-up with plancha on top of the stainless steel grid.

TARGET TEMP
180°C/350°F

TORTILLAS

In Mexican kitchens, tortillas are cooked on a 'comal', a hotplate that's very similar to the plancha in your EGG. This will make for interesting scorching on the surface, will render the shortening that the dough was made with and will steam through the core of the tortilla. It is essential that you keep them warm afterwards though, and try to prevent steam from escaping, or the tortillas will become hard and chewy. The best way to keep them in good condition is with a proprietary tortilla box – the kind of drum-shaped plastic job you may have seen at a Mexican restaurant, or in a padded bag, much like our own tea-cosy, or wrapped in clean dry dish towels.

Mix the masa harina and salt in a bowl. Slowly add the water and mix until a dough forms and you can shape it into a ball, then knead a few times with your hands. Add more water or flour to give a pliable dough that isn't sticky.

Divide the dough into pieces and roll into balls. Place a dough ball between two pieces of parchment paper. Use a tortilla press, plate or heavy pan to flatten the ball into a circle. (You can use a rolling pin, but it might fray a bit at the edges.) Carefully peel off the paper.

Burp and open the EGG. Place as many tortillas as will fit onto a preheated plancha or cast-iron skillet. It might take you a few tries to get the hang of it, depending on your set-up, but start by cooking the first side for 30 seconds, lift an edge with a spatula to check if the heat is starting to brown the surface, then once you see mottling or the tortilla starts to inflate a little from the internal steam, flip and cook for another minute on the other side.

Stack into your box, padded bag/tea-cosy or dish towel, covering immediately to retain the steam. Repeat until all your tortillas are cooked, then flip the whole stack over, so the ones that were cooked first are on top, and rush to the table as fast as possible.

You'll need as many tortillas as you think you might reasonably need, plus about half as many again. Once they get started, people don't seem to stop.

Makes 15

250g masa harina
300ml tepid water
Pinch of salt, to taste

EGG SET UP
Direct set-up with the plancha or with the grid with cast-iron skillet on top.

TARGET TEMP
190–210°C/
375–410°F

AÏOLI MONSTRE

The Aïoli 'Monstre' is one of the great performative feasts of the French hospitality industry, and like the Couscous 'Royale' and the equally monstrous 'Choucroute Garni', it's brought to the table on a huge platter, an oversize demonstration of hospitality and generosity. French cooking being what it is, though, the traditional aïoli monstre involves ingredients that have been poached in a court bouillon or stock. These are lovely and subtle things but they are infinitely improved by grilling, developing the extra flavours of the Maillard reaction, caramelization and even charring. Aïoli originates in the South of France, near the border with Spain, or more particularly, Cataluña, where they have their own noble traditions of dipping vegetables: the calçotada is a feast, often involving a whole town, which simply celebrates grilling leeks on the fire and eating them dipped in a special pepper-based emulsion sauce. They also have their own characteristic ways with salted fish.

To the utter dismay of any Catalan or Provençal purists, this feast steals freely from both culinary traditions. It can easily be adapted to be entirely vegetarian. It's worth mentioning that this feast also comprises some versatile sauces, the absolute Master Recipe for chicken roasting, and a method that works with almost any vegetables. Definitely worth getting into your EGGmaster's repertoire.

One last thought... if you worry about time management when cooking for large groups, everything here is great served hot, even better warm and absolutely lovely cold, so you shouldn't need to break a sweat.

SERVES 6–8

FEAST MENU

AÏOLI:
20–30 minutes cooking time
160–180°C/320–350°F

ROMESCO SAUCE:
15–25 minutes cooking time
160–180°C/320–350°F

GRILLED LEEKS:
25 minutes cooking time
160–180°C/320–350°F

ROAST CHICKEN:
45–60 minutes cooking time
160–180°C/320–350°F

GRILLED SALT COD/BACALAO:
15–20 minutes cooking time
180°C/350°F

ROAST VEGETABLES:
10 minutes cooking time
160–180°C/320–350°F

EGG FEAST SET UP
(if cooking everything together as a feast)

Load and light your EGG. Bring it to 180°C/ 350°F and add the convEGGtor basket with half moon plancha, half moon baking stone bottom right, stainless steel grid top right and a multi-level grid. If using a MiniMax bring it to 180°C/350°F, cook the sauce components directly on the stainless steel grid first, then add in the convEGGtor and stainless steel grid back on top to roast the rest, dish after dish.

FEAST METHOD
(if cooking everything together as a feast)

1   Make the aïoli on the half moon stainless steel grid.

2   Make the romesco on the half moon plancha, or half moon searing grid.

3   Put the chicken on the stainless steel grid, remove the half moon plancha and add a drip tray underneath on the baking stone; add a small glass of wine from Provence to the pan so the chicken juice does not burn. Place the half moon plancha (or half moon searing grid) back on the left.

4   Add the multi-level rack and place the salt cod/bacalao in a small pan on the multi-level above.

5   Grill the leeks on the half moon plancha (or half moon searing grid).

6   Remove the roasting pan and add the vegetables to the roasting pan with the chicken juice, then roast on the stainless steel grid.

NOTES

1   Desalinate the cod beforehand (see page 173).

2   Remember to burp your EGG when opening at high temperatures and cook with the dome closed.

3   Make sure you prepare your sauces in advance according to the feast running order.

4   You can cook all of these dishes one after the other.

AÏOLI

Of all the garlicky mayonnaise-like preparations around southern France and northern Spain, Provençal aïoli is the easiest to love. It has egg yolk as its base and includes a little French mustard – which usefully makes it much easier to make and much less likely to split. You can increase the amount of olive oil you use instead of some of the sunflower oil, if you prefer.

Wrap the whole garlic head in a sheet of foil brushed with olive oil, burp and open your preheated EGG, then cook for 20–30 minutes with the dome closed until softened. Squeeze the flesh out and leave to cool.

Whisk together the egg yolks, mustard, garlic flesh, a big pinch of salt and a little black pepper in a bowl.

Put the oils into a jug that is easy to pour from, then slowly start whisking a few drops of oil into the egg mix.

Slowly increase the quantity of oil added each time, whisking in each addition so it is properly amalgamated, before adding the next. Once the sauce has started to hold its shape, you can start to add the oil in a thin stream.

When you have added all the oil, you should have a thick and wobbly aïoli that holds its shape. Whisk in half a dozen drops of cold water.

Taste and check the seasoning and add a little vinegar and salt. Cover and refrigerate if not using immediately.

Makes about 500ml/2 cups

1 large head of garlic
2 large, free-range egg yolks
15g/½oz Dijon mustard
100ml/scant ½ cup extra-virgin olive oil, plus extra for brushing
300ml/generous 1¼ cups sunflower oil
Vinegar, to taste
Salt and freshly ground black pepper

EGG SET UP
Direct set-up with the stainless steel grid in place.

TARGET TEMP
160–180°C/320–350°F

ROMESCO SAUCE

Makes about 500ml/2 cups

1 red (bell) pepper

3 ripe tomatoes

1 head of garlic

1 slice of sourdough bread, crusts removed

2 dried ñora peppers, stems and seeds removed and soaked in warm water for about 5 minutes

30g/1oz hazelnuts

1 tbsp red wine vinegar or sherry vinegar, plus more to taste

60ml/¼ cup extra-virgin olive oil

Salt and freshly ground black pepper

Romesco is a sauce from the Spanish side of the Pyrenees that characteristically uses bread rather than eggs as a thickening agent for oil, garlic and fruity (bell) peppers. This particular recipe is not classic – the trick with the garlicky toast comes from Salvitxada, the sauce made in Catalonia, solely for use with grilled leeks.

Burp and open the preheated EGG and grill the red pepper, tomatoes and garlic (except for one reserved clove) for 15–25 minutes, with the dome closed, until soft.

Burp your EGG, remove the pepper and set aside. Add the sourdough bread to the grid, turning regularly to develop a nice char, remove from the EGG and close the dome. Rub the spare clove of garlic over the toasted surface. You'll be amazed how fast it's grated and absorbed.

Peel the grilled pepper (and deseed) and the tomatoes and squeeze the soft garlic flesh out of its skin. Drain the ñora peppers and add to the vegetables.

Blend the toast, hazelnuts, vegetable mix and vinegar together and process until the mixture is smooth. Gradually add the olive oil in a thin stream until it is fully emulsified. Season with salt and pepper, plus more vinegar if you like.

EGG SET UP
Direct set-up with the plancha or cast-iron searing grid.

TARGET TEMP
160–180°C/320–350°F

GRILLED LEEKS

Serves 2–4

6 leeks

The calçot is a type of allium grown in Cataluña under EU regional protections, and it is vitally important that they are not in any way mistaken for small tender leeks. They do taste, however, remarkably like small and tender leeks and are so peculiarly delicate and delicious when they're scorched on the outside so their insides steam, that the Catalans throw vast festivals for their sole consumption. This recipe is emphatically for grilled leeks.

Burp and open the preheated EGG and cook the leeks on the grill for 20–25 minutes, with the dome closed, until the outsides are charred and the leeks are softened. Burp the EGG, remove the leeks and leave until cool enough to handle.

Cut off the root end of each leek, then run a sharp knife down the length of the leek. Peel away and discard the blackened layers and remove the soft middle.

EGG SET UP
Direct set-up with the cast-iron grid in place or half moon plancha.

TARGET TEMP
160–180°C/320–350°F

ROAST CHICKEN

There's nothing particularly regional or authentic about this recipe but you might find it the most useful in the book. This is the simplest way to roast any amount of jointed chicken – you don't need to vary the times as much as you might when calculating the size of a whole bird, so it's a much more forgiving way to roast and ensures that the legs are cooked fully but the breast meat isn't dried out. The juices are also sublime. This is definitely one to have in your repertoire.

Rub salt and pepper all over the chicken pieces, then lay them out in a single layer in a roasting tray (or trays) skin-side down, drizzle with the olive oil and scatter over the garlic, bay leaves and thyme. Burp and open your preheated EGG and cook for about 45–60 minutes with the dome closed until cooked through (the internal temperature should be about 75°C/167°F).

Burp the EGG, remove the chicken from the tray(s), carefully reserving the fats and juices (you'll use these to cook the vegetables in – see page 175), and leave to cool.

Once cool enough to handle, remove the skin and bones and slice and pull the meat into 2cm/¾in-thick strips, then give it an extra grind of black pepper and serve at room temperature.

Serves 4–6

1 large free-range chicken, jointed but on the bone

30ml/2 tbsp olive oil

6 garlic cloves, squashed but left whole

2 bay leaves

2 large sprigs of thyme

Salt and freshly ground black pepper

EGG SET UP
Indirect set-up; the convEGGtor in the legs-up position with the stainless steel grid on top of the convEGGtor legs. Drip pan with optional vertical chicken roaster.

TARGET TEMP
160–180°C/320–350°F

GRILLED SALT COD/BACALAO

Salt cod is one of the traditional ingredients of the French aïoli monstre, but in its Spanish form – bacalao – it's often served with Romesco sauce. Salt cod worries some diners who feel that preserved fish will be somehow salty or unpleasant, but they shouldn't worry. After two days of soaking, the cod tastes amazing, with a slightly intensified flavour when compared to totally fresh cod. If you wish, you can take the opposite approach and brine fresh white fish in salt for a few hours. This, again, enhances the flavour and tightens the texture.

It does depend on how salty and dry the fish is, but to desalinate salt cod, soak it in cold water, changing every few hours, for 12–36 hours. Just taste a little bit (it's fine to eat raw) every now and then.

Rub the pieces of fish with olive oil. Place them in a pan, skin-side down, and place in the preheated EGG.

Cook for 15–25 minutes with the dome closed until the fish's internal temperature is about 45°C/115°F.

Leave to rest and serve at room temperature.

Serves 4

4 loin pieces of salt cod with skin (about 800g/1lb 12oz total weight), desalinated (or use fresh cod that you've brined)

Olive oil

EGG SET UP
Indirect set-up; the convEGGtor in the legs-up position with the stainless steel grid on top of the convEGGtor legs. Use either a skillet or a Big Green Egg paella pan.

TARGET TEMP
180–200°C/ 350–400°F

ROAST VEGETABLES

These vegetables are grilled for added flavour, but the EGG enables you to add even more flavour. Because of the enclosed, dry 'baking' heat, you can add a kind of glaze/marinade to the surface of the veg, like you would with a piece of meat or fish. This particular combination of ingredients is designed to have a kind of gluey consistency so it holds to the surface of the veg. And please don't worry if you can't stand Marmite or English mustard. Both flavours 'cook out' of the marinade, leaving only a browning effect and a deep extra note of umami. Remember to burp your EGG when opening at high temperatures and keep the dome closed when cooking.

Make the Marmite seasoning mix. Mix the Marmite with the mustard powder in a bowl. Grate in the garlic and stir in the oregano, then let down the paste with the oil.

Toss all of the vegetables individually in the Marmite mix.

Open the preheated EGG. If cooking for the feast, return the chicken tray(s) containing all the reserved fats and juices (see page 171) to the EGG to heat the juices directly on the grill. If cooking individually, move on to the next step.

In batches, open the EGG, add the veg and cook for about 2–8 minutes with the dome closed, adding 100ml/3½fl oz of the chicken/marmite seasoning liquid to each batch and cooking until it's absorbed, has evaporated and the vegetables are tender. Each vegetable will cook in a different amount of time, so keep checking and turning everything.

Serve the grilled veg with the chicken.

Serves 6–8

2 fennel bulbs, each cut into 6
2 bunches of asparagus, trimmed
300g/10½oz green beans, trimmed
400g/14oz small carrots, cut in half lengthways
Salt and freshly ground black pepper

For the Marmite seasoning mix
10g/¼oz Marmite
5g/⅙oz English mustard powder
3 garlic cloves, peeled
Pinch of dried oregano
20g/¾oz olive oil
Freshly ground black pepper

EGG SET UP
Direct set-up with the plancha or baking stone on top of the stainless steel grid. If using the chicken juices in the drip pan you will need to continue with an indirect set-up; the convEGGtor in the legs-up position with the stainless steel grid on top of the convEGGtor legs.

TARGET TEMP
180°C/350°F

GAMES NIGHT

The kind of snacks associated with spectator sports have, historically, been quite frightening. Terrifying pies, unspeakable meats in various forms of bun, and sausages more useful as missiles than sustenance. Fortunately, things have changed. These days you can have your friends round to watch it all on widescreen, wheel out the EGG and enjoy some far more sophisticated stuff. Do please note that these are equally appropriate if your game of choice is Dominoes, Cards, Dungeons & Dragons or Catan – hell, they're even good for Book Club – and that whole smoked cabbage can still be used as a weapon if things get argumentative.

SERVES 10–14

FEAST MENU

PASTRAMI: 6-9 hours cooking time 120°C/250°F

PRESSED RIB DIP SARNIE: overnight cooking time 130–150°C/265–300°F then 160–200°C/320–400°F

MEATBALLS: 45 minutes cooking time 180–200°C/350–400°F then 200–220°C/400–425°F

VEGETABLE BURNT ENDS: 45 minutes cooking time 160–180°C/320–350°F

SMOKED WHOLE CABBAGE: 30 minutes cooking time 170–200°C/325–400°F

PØLSEN: 5 minutes cooking time 200°C/400°F

HOT CARAMELIZED FRUIT AND CUSTARD: 15 minutes cooking time 150–180°C/300–350°F

EGG FEAST SET UP
(if cooking everything together as a feast)

THE DAY BEFORE
Load and light your EGG; target temperature is 130–150°C/265–300°F. You will need to set up for indirect cooking, with the convEGGtor and stainless steel grid on top.

ON THE DAY
Load and light your EGG; target temperature is 120°C/250°F. You will need to set up for indirect cooking, with the convEGGtor and stainless steel grid on top.

Then you will need to set up with the EGGspander for direct and indirect cooking; target temperature is 180–200°C/350–400°F. Add the convEGGtor basket with the half moon stainless steel grid top left with the plancha on top, half moon cast-iron searing grid top right and a multi-level grid.

FEAST METHOD
(if cooking everything together as a feast)

1   Prepare the pastrami (5–7 days before).

2   Cook and chill the rib sandwich overnight on Games Night eve.

3   On the day of Games Night, prepare and cook the pastrami.

4   Cook the meatballs.

5   Cook the vegetable burnt ends at the same time as the meatballs.

6   Smoke the cabbage at the same time as the meatballs and burnt ends. Remove the three dishes; eat or keep warm.

7   Finish the rib sandwich.

8   Cook the hot dogs at the same time as the rib sandwich.

9   Cook the fruit and custard.

PASTRAMI

Pastrami is the pride of the New York Jewish deli. The reason, I hope it isn't disrespectful to observe, is that it has all the phenomenal deliciousness of bacon or ham while remaining resolutely kosher. It requires, let's face it, a long and involved cooking process, but it's worth every second of the work. Hot, fresh pastrami in a sandwich or roll is one of the high points of human culinary achievement, exceeded only by the spectacular delight of an enormous amount, cold, the day after. Make plenty.

Combine all the brine ingredients in a saucepan with 2L/ 8¾ cups of water. Bring to the boil and then leave to cool. Your pickling spice mixture should be a closely guarded personal secret, but I use a mixture of mace, allspice, juniper, coriander, ginger, dried chillies and just a couple of cloves. You can go wherever you fancy with this.

Pack the whole brisket into two large, doubled-up, zip-seal freezer bags (the brisket goes in the inner bag of the two). Ladle in the brine, exclude as much air as you can, then seal both bags. Place in the fridge and turn daily for at least 5 days, but preferably 7 days.

Remove the brisket and pat it dry with paper towels. Crush the peppercorns and coriander seeds roughly, then massage them hard into the surface of the brisket, trying to get as much to adhere as possible.

Burp and open your preheated EGG and add in smoking wood chunks of your choice – hickory or oak works well with beef. Now set up for indirect cooking, with your convEGGtor in a legs up position with the stainless steel grid on top. The temperature will drop; do not play with your vents and it will regulate back to the target temperature. You will need to act quickly. It is not easy to bring your EGG's temperature down to such a low temperature if a lot of oxygen is being added, as it will increase the temperature dramatically the longer you leave it open. Place the brisket straight onto the grid and cook for 3–5 hours with the dome closed, chucking handfuls of wood or wood chips onto the fire every 1½ hours to keep it good and smoky. You'll want to end with the brisket's internal temperature of 70°C/158°F.

Put your smoked brisket in a roasting tray on a rack over about 5cm/2in of boiling water, then build a foil tent around it and seal it up. Try to keep as much free space around the meat as possible for the steam to circulate. Put it back into the EGG at 120°C/250°F for about 3–4 hours until the internal temperature is about 93°/199°F. A fork should slide into it like butter.

Serves 6–8

For the basic brine
200g/7oz salt

75g/generous ⅓ cup granulated sugar

15g/½oz Prague Powder #1 (optional)

2 bay leaves

2 garlic cloves, peeled

50g/1¾oz honey

15g/½oz pickling spice

For the pastrami
2kg/4lb 8oz brisket

10g/¼oz black peppercorns

10g/¼oz coriander seeds

Handful of Hickory or Oak smoking chunks

Boiling water

EGG SET UP
Indirect set-up; the convEGGtor in the legs-up position with the stainless steel grid or cast-iron grid on top of the convEGGtor legs.

TARGET TEMP
120–140°C/ 250–275°F

PRESSED RIB DIP SANDWICH

Serves 4

3-rib slab of beef short-rib

1 large white onion, sliced

3 garlic cloves, crushed

½ red or green chilli, deseeded and roughly chopped

5g/½ oz dried oregano

½ bottle red wine

80g/2¾oz olive oil

Freshly ground black pepper, to taste

To serve
100ml/scant ½ cup chicken stock

6 small baguettes

Olive oil, for brushing

Dijon mustard, for spreading

2 heads of Little Gem lettuce, separated into leaves

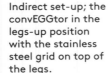

EGG SET UP
Indirect set-up; the convEGGtor in the legs-up position with the stainless steel grid on top of the legs.

TARGET TEMP
130–150°C/265–300°F

Then...
Direct set-up with the stainless steel grid and cast-iron plancha.

TARGET TEMP
160–200°C/320–400°F

This is one of those dishes you can prepare alongside a regular cook on the EGG but which creates the amazing base component of this recipe. The meat needs a night or more in the fridge so it can be finished in the kitchen or on the EGG later. The idea of pressing and re-cooking braised meat crops up in different cuisines all over the world, but the final presentation in this case is based on a Portuguese sandwich called a Prego that used to be served at the Eagle – London's first gastropub.

The day before you intend to cook, find yourself an ovenproof vessel into which the rib will just fit and put all the ingredients in, cover and leave to marinate in the fridge overnight.

Using the indirect set-up, burp and open your preheated EGG, leave the meat in its marinade and bring it up to a simmer. If it starts to boil too rapidly, just cover it with foil and adjust your vents to decrease the temperature. Turn the heat off, cover the meat and leave it cooling in its marinade in the cooling EGG, either overnight or for the rest of the day.

Slip the bones out of the meat, wrap it tightly in cling film (plastic wrap) and put a chopping board on top and a few cans or a big casserole to weight it down, then put it in the fridge overnight. Store the marinade and vegetables separately in the fridge. You can freeze both the meat and the marinade at this point, then one dark winter night when you're craving a great meat feast, Future You will thank Today You for your prescience.

Bring your EGG up to temperature in the direct set-up, unwrap the chilled meat and carve it into thick slices. Burp your EGG, bring the marinade to a simmer in a pan on the plancha, add the chicken stock and reduce to a thin gravy; close the dome.

Split the baguettes and paint the cut faces with olive oil, then burp the EGG and grill the meat slices on the bars or on the plancha. However you choose to do it, sear the meat on both sides. You're looking for a nice crust. 'Butter' the baguettes with mustard, add a layer of lettuce leaves and then the meat.

Use a slotted spoon to dredge out the stewed and soft onion slices and chilli pieces and pile them on top of the meat. Now you can a) spoon the gravy over the sandwiches b) serve the gravy in a big bowl for dipping c) both.

MEATBALLS

Serves 4

3 Italian salsicce (sausages),
fennel-flavoured

100g/1¼ cups stale white breadcrumbs

250g/9oz minced (ground) beef

7 garlic cloves, peeled

Pinch of fennel seeds

Pinch of garlic powder

1 large dried allspice berry

75g/2½oz crème fraîche

1 egg

3 x 400g/14oz cans tomatoes

Salt and freshly ground black pepper

Plenty of grated Parmesan cheese,
to serve

EGG SET UP
Direct set-up with
the stainless steel
grid or cast-iron grid.

TARGET TEMP
180–200°C/350–400°F

Then...
Indirect set-up; the
convEGGtor in the
legs-up position
with the stainless
steel grid on top of
the legs.

TARGET TEMP
200–220°C/400–425°F

Most recipes recommend that meat be seared and 'sealed' before cooking in liquids so their flavours can be retained. Meatballs are the entire opposite. No matter what anyone tells you, never grill, roast or fry your meatballs. Make a plain tomato sauce in which they can be poached and then maybe brown the surface a little at the end if you must. The meatballs should leak and flavour the sauce, the sauce must penetrate and enhance the meatballs. It is only this unique blending that can make meatballs in tomato sauce greater than the sum of its parts. Remember to burp your EGG when opening at high temperatures and cook with the dome closed.

Skin the sausages and break them up into a bowl. Stir in the breadcrumbs and combine thoroughly before adding the minced beef. Grate in three of the garlic cloves, then add the fennel seeds and garlic powder. Grate or crush the allspice berry and add. Stir in the crème fraîche and egg, then with wet hands, roll the mix into smooth balls, each the size of an egg.

Pour the canned tomatoes into a flat, open, ovenproof dish or skillet along with the remaining garlic cloves. Open your preheated EGG and cook for 8–12 minutes, until the sauce is reduced and the top is scorched. Remove from the EGG, season with salt and pepper and blitz with a stick blender.

Using the indirect set-up, sink the meatballs carefully into the tomato sauce, then return to the EGG, with the dome closed, allowing the meatballs to poach in the sauce and the flavours to exchange, for about 30 minutes. A very small amount of smoking chips added to the charcoal before adding in the convEGGtor will add a subtle smokiness.

Carefully roll the meatballs with a spoon, so the underside gets a bit of exposure and perhaps try another tiny puff of smoke. Once you reach this final stage, don't stir or disturb again, allowing the top to crust a little and perhaps blacken a bit here and there (with a core temperature of 75°C/167°F or over).

Remove the pan and spoon out over cooked pasta or a split baguette, and top with loads of Parmesan to serve.

VEGETABLE BURNT ENDS

Serves 6

1 swede (rutabaga) (b)

½ cauliflower (b)

Broccoli (b), Brussels sprouts (b)
kohlrabi (b) (optional)

4 carrots

1 celeriac (celery root)

2 parsnips

1 butternut squash

15g/½oz Marmite

1 tbsp olive oil

15g/½oz English mustard powder

10g/¼oz porcini powder

5g/⅛oz salt

5g/⅛oz garlic powder

5g/⅛oz ground black pepper

5g/⅛oz sweet smoked paprika

5g/⅛oz dried thyme or oregano

natural (plain) yoghurt or crème
fraîche, to serve (optional)

(b) = brassica

EGG SET UP
Indirect set-up
with a roasting
pan (drip pan),
the stainless steel
grid on top of the
convEGGtor legs.

TARGET TEMP
160–180°C/320–
350°F

Roast vegetables are always a good thing, but in the last few years, chefs have started to notice something new. Roast veg can be improved by a little judicious charring. It's a technique that needs to be applied carefully if you're not just going to end up with carbonized biomass, but it's worth the effort. This combination is based on the old BBQ favourite of 'Burnt Ends', where sweet, juicy and umami meat is enhanced by 'overcooking'. The brassicas here have bitterness and a strong enough flavour to stand up to a proper torching. Carrots, sweet potatoes, onions and butternut squash are sweet, so they need the help of what you might call a scorching mix, which adds both flavour notes and 'catches' a little to promote charring. Remember to burp your EGG when opening at high temperatures and cook with the dome closed.

Peel (and deseed) your veg and separate out the brassicas. Imagine a 4cm/1½in cube. Cut or trim all the veg into chunks or florets that would fit into it. This is not an exact science but we're trying to control things so everything cooks evenly.

In the bottom of your roasting pan, dissolve the Marmite in a splash of boiling water, then stir in the olive oil. Use a pestle and mortar or a grinder to combine and crush all the dry ingredients into a powder.

Roll the non-brassicas about in the Marmitey liquid until they're thoroughly and stickily coated, then sprinkle over the flavouring powder and toss enthusiastically. Everything should have a good coating, and now add the brassicas. The idea here is that the flavouring should mainly adhere to the places where it's most needed. If there's no free liquid in the base of the roasting pan, add a splash of water or beer (you need bitter flavours here). Cover loosely with foil, and place in the preheated EGG. After 10 minutes, remove the foil.

After another 10 minutes cooking, the top of the veg should be starting to brown and any liquid in the pan should have evaporated down to a sludge. Use a large spoon or spatula to scrape the veg off the pan and roll them over.

For the last 10 minutes, keep an eye on the veg. They will begin to brown and scorch nicely, but pay them the same attention you would a serious piece of meat. Turn or remove anything that looks like it's going too far. Rest the veg for 5 minutes under the foil. There's plenty of flavour here so we won't need much else, maybe a spoonful of natural yoghurt or crème fraîche, if you feel it's appropriate.

SMOKED WHOLE CABBAGE

Serves 4

150g/5½oz Gorgonzola cheese

100g/3½oz soured (sour) cream

100g/3½oz mayonnaise

50g/1¾oz horseradish sauce

Pinch of chilli flakes (red pepper flakes)

Shot of Worcestershire sauce

1 whole cabbage – white, green, red or hispi

100g/7 tbsp butter, cut into cubes

½ garlic clove, crushed

75g/2½oz whole blanched hazelnuts

Salt and freshly ground black pepper

Handful of water-soaked pecan smoking chips

A whole cabbage, grilled on the EGG is a wonderful quick win, but you can improve on it by a combination method of steaming for texture, grilling for delicious char and smoking and basting for complexity. Remember to burp your EGG when opening at high temperatures and cook with the dome closed.

Combine the cheese, soured cream, mayo and horseradish sauce in a bowl and use a fork to smush the cheese into irregular lumps. Season with the chilli flakes and the Worcestershire sauce. Set aside.

Use a small, sharp knife to cut the core out of the cabbage, leaving a neat, conical hole. Season heavily with salt and pepper.

Before adding the convEGGtor, add in your soaked wood chips.

Wrap the cabbage in foil. Arrange so the cabbage will stand upside down, with the foil left open at the top to reveal the conical hole. Put the wrapped cabbage onto the bars of the preheated EGG and drop in the butter cubes and garlic.

Cook the cabbage gently with the dome closed until the butter has melted and you can see steam rising from the open top of the foil. Close the foil and continue to cook for 10 minutes.

Open the EGG. Remove and unwrap the cabbage and place it, hole-side down, in a metal baking dish or small skillet. A fair bit of butter should run out into the dish/skillet. If it doesn't, place a bit more on the top of the cabbage, then burp and add back to the EGG; let the butter melt.

Open the dome and baste the cabbage with the melted butter, then add a small amount of smoking chips to the charcoal and close the dome. After 5 minutes, lift the dome and then baste again.

Continue cooking and basting the cabbage until the outside leaves are deep brown and glossy, about 30 minutes.

Meanwhile, toast the hazelnuts in a dry skillet, alongside the cabbage or on the hob, then cool slightly and crush coarsely. Cut the cabbage into wedges and serve dressed with the last of the pan butter, topped with the blue cheese cream and sprinkled with the nut crumb.

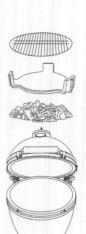

EGG SET UP
Indirect set-up; the convEGGtor in the legs-up position with the stainless steel grid or cast-iron grid on top of the convEGGtor legs.

TARGET TEMP
170–200°C/325–400°F

PØLSEN – SCANDI HOT DOGS

Serves 4–8

4–8 hot dog sausages of your choice

olive oil, for cooking

4–8 regular white hot dog buns, split in half

For the pickles

1 small cucumber

20g/¾oz dill fronds, torn

10g/¼oz sugar

10g/¼oz salt

5g/⅛oz coriander seeds

5g/⅛oz black peppercorns

200ml/¾ cup white pickling vinegar

100g/3½oz crisp deep-fried onions

For the remoulade

8 cornichons

1 pickled gherkin (sweet)

½ red chilli, deseeded

100g/3½oz piccalilli

100g/3½oz mayonnaise

Salt and freshly ground black pepper

For the prawn (shrimp) cocktail

100g/3½oz small cooked peeled prawns (shrimp)

75g/2½oz Japanese mayonnaise

25g/1oz tomato ketchup

10g/¼oz horseradish sauce

Pinch of smoked paprika

Lemon juice, to taste

Think of a summer cookout and most people will think of hot dogs. It's true that a big old sausage is at the heart of the grill tradition from the US to SA, from the UK to Australia. But quietly, I reckon, it's the Scandinavians who've become the nation to watch when it comes to hot dogs. In Denmark, Norway and Sweden, hot dog carts are a fixture of the night-time street scene. We would instantly recognize the good steamed pølsen (sausages) and the cheap, fluffy bun, but it's what they put on top that's a game changer. So buy your favourite hot dog sausages wherever you like, be they bratwurst, frankfurters, kielbasa or even a standard banger. Pick up your regular hot dog rolls, grill them gently on the EGG, and try serving them in one of these three ways.

Good-quality hot dog sausages are available from supermarkets, sometimes packed in jars of brine. I've recently been finding even better ones in specialist Polish grocers. Kielbasa are flavoured with garlic and can be smoked. As with a good burger, I find it important that the bun be of quite low quality. This is certainly no place for sourdough, brioche or anything artisanal. A hot dog bun should be very soft, very white and ideally mass-produced.

For the pickles, slice the cucumber finely and pack into a clean jar, layering with the torn dill fronds. Put the sugar, salt, coriander seeds and peppercorns in a small pan with the vinegar and bring quickly to the boil. Leave to cool a little before pouring over the cucumber. Make sure everything is covered before sealing the lid, cooling and storing in the fridge for 5 days.

For the remoulade sauce, chop the cornichons, gherkin and chilli into the finest micro-dice you can manage. Use a fork to roughly crush most of the lumps in the piccalilli, then combine all the ingredients in a bowl and adjust the seasoning to taste.

For the prawn cocktail, cut each prawn into about four chunky little slices. Combine all the ingredients in a bowl, carefully folding them together with a silicone spatula. Adjust the seasoning to taste.

continued overleaf...

Massage the hot dog sausages with a little oil, just to stop them sticking to the bars. Burp and open the preheated EGG and grill the sausages, moving them around to pick up a few attractive splits and grill marks just before serving.

I prefer not to toast the buns. For me, the sweetness and texture of an absolutely crappy, shop-bought bun is a vital part of the experience of a great hot dog. Also make sure you buy the regular-sized one no matter how vast your sausage. The Scandi way seems to be to use the bun merely as a handling tool for the main event... pølsen and topping.

The prawn cocktail should be laid reverently along the top of the sausage and possibly dusted with a little extra paprika to make the colour even more alarming.

The pickles are traditionally combined with a generous sprinkling of crisp deep-fried onions. Not the fresh ones but those weird, dry, store cupboard ones you can find in IKEA, which I suspect might actually be a by-product of wood machining. The remoulade is good enough to just be trowelled on by itself.

EGG SET UP
Direct set-up with the stainless steel grid or cast-iron grid.

TARGET TEMP
200°C/400°F

HOT CARAMELIZED FRUIT AND CUSTARD

Serves 4–8

For the custard

300ml/generous 1½ cups full-fat (whole) milk, plus 1 tbsp extra for the cornflour (cornstarch)

300ml/generous 1½ cups double (heavy) cream

50g/1¾oz honey

1 sprig of thyme, plus another sprig with leaves picked (for the fruit)

1 tbsp cornflour (cornstarch)

5 egg yolks

For the fruit

100g/½ cup demerara or soft light brown sugar

Pinch of salt

12 smallish plums, cut in half and pitted

50ml/3½ tablespoons Marsala, Madeira or sweet sherry

50g/3½ tbsp butter

Crushed amaretti biscuits or ground almonds, to serve

EGG SET UP
Direct set-up with the stainless steel grid or cast-iron grid.

TARGET TEMP
150–180°C/300–350°F

Except in the very hottest summer months, caramelized fruit and custard is my absolute go-to EGG dessert. Whatever fruit is in season can be caramelized and – this is a terrible admission! – will taste absolutely superb with cold, canned custard. I can particularly recommend serving plums, apricots or figs in this way. This recipe, though, is the posh version, with extremely refined and cheffy custard, made from scratch and lightly seared on top at the last minute before bringing it to the table. Remember to burp your EGG when opening at high temperatures and keep the dome closed when cooking.

Make the custard. Warm the milk, cream, honey and whole thyme sprig in a medium saucepan and bring it slowly to the boil. Remove from the heat and leave to infuse for 10 minutes.

In a cup, blend the cornflour with the tablespoon of milk until smooth.

Whisk the egg yolks in a heatproof bowl until pale. Strain the warm milk/cream mixture into the egg yolks, stirring it constantly until well combined. Tip the mixture back into the saucepan and warm over a low-medium heat.

Cook for 10 minutes or so, stirring constantly, until the custard is thick enough to coat the back of a wooden spoon, then remix the cornflour mixture and stir it into the custard. Cook for a couple of minutes more, stirring constantly until thick. Remove it from the heat and cover with a damp dish towel.

For the fruit, mix together the sugar and salt on a large plate, then press the cut side of each plum into the sugar mixture to coat.

Open your preheated EGG and heat up a large skillet, then add the sugar-coated plums, cut-side down, and cook, with the dome closed, until the sugar and juices caramelize, about 3–4 minutes. As the fruit caramelizes, turn it over, adding the fortified wine, thyme leaves and butter, then cook for 30 seconds until it has evaporated and the butter is bubbling.

Remove the skillet. Pour the custard over the plums, sprinkle on the crushed amaretti or ground almonds, then return to the EGG for a few minutes to brown a little on the surface.

WINTER WARMERS

It seems a shame that we restrict our outdoor cooking to a relatively limited summer 'season'. It's true that it seems easier to consider outdoor eating when your lips aren't blue with cold and your woolly mittens aren't absorbing grease. But some of my happiest times with the EGG have been on crisp days in late autumn or winter – wrapped up properly, yes, but also warmed by the heat of the EGG as I cook. The EGG, with its slow cooking and controllable smoke, really lends itself to autumn and winter foods. In the UK, we have Bonfire Night in November, we increasingly share Halloween with the US and, of course, Americans have their own Thanksgiving. All excuses to cook up the perfect winter feast.

SERVES 8–12

FEAST MENU
BEEF RIB CHILLI: 1½–2 hours cooking time 140–160°C/275–320°F

SLOW ROAST CELERIAC 'JOINT': 2 hours cooking time 140–160°C/275–320°F then 200–220°C/400–425°F

BRAISED OR SALT-BAKED BEETROOT SALAD: 1 hour cooking time 180–200°C/350–400°F

CREAM-FILLED BABY SQUASH: 50–65 minutes cooking time 180–200°C/325–400°F

CORN 'FONDANT': 30–40 minutes cooking time 150–180°C/300–350°F

CHOCOLATE GRILLED SANDWICHES: 1½ minutes cooking time 150–180°C/300–350°F

EGG FEAST SET UP
(if cooking everything together as a feast)

Load and light your EGG. Bring it to 150–160°C/300–320°F and add the convEGGtor basket, the convEGGtor in the legs-up position and the stainless steel grid on top with the multi-level grid needed later. You will also need a cast-iron plancha for pud!

FEAST METHOD
(if cooking everything together as a feast)

1   Start the beef chilli.

2   Once the wet ingredients are in with the chilli, add the celeriac joint on the stainless steel grid alongside it.

3   Add the beetroot in a pan on the multi-level grid above or alongside the chilli.

4   Remove the beetroot and keep warm. Add in the squash.

5   Remove the chilli and celeriac and keep warm until needed.

6   Increase the EGG temperature to 180–200°C/350–400°F. Add the corn fondant.

7   Assemble the beetroot salad.

8   Remove the squash. Add in the cast-iron plancha to heat up whilst you serve the feast. Cook the chocolate grilled sandwiches on top of the plancha.

NOTE
Cook to temperature and not time. The short rib needs long and slow cooking at a low temperature. It's ready when it's ready.

BEEF RIB CHILLI

Serves 4

2 tsp ground cumin

½ tsp ground allspice

1 tsp salt, plus extra for seasoning

½ tsp freshly ground black pepper,
plus extra for seasoning

1kg/2lb 4oz beef ribs, or ox cheeks

2 onions, finely chopped

4 garlic cloves, finely chopped

2 tbsp dripping or vegetable oil

2 bay leaves

½ cinnamon stick

1 tsp Mexican dried oregano

2–3 small chipotles in adobo,
finely chopped (or 2–3 tsp ground
chipotles)

200g/7oz tomato passata (puréed
tomatoes)

1 tsp red or white wine vinegar

2 tsp sugar or honey

Salt and freshly ground black pepper

Hot sauce, to serve

Look up 'chilli con carne' on the internet and you'll discover some useful things. Firstly, nobody in Mexico would ever call this famously Mexican dish Chile con Carne, and secondly, you'll discover that, though the dish doesn't really exist, there are a million or so massively varying recipes for it, each more aggressively defended as 'authentic' than the last. Like chicken tikka masala and spaghetti Bolognese, chilli is now a phenomenally successful dish internationally. You need a fantastic chilli in your repertoire, this is just ours... where you take it next is entirely up to you. When shopping for the beef ribs, order short ribs that are usually 4 ribs in one rack with the bone at the bottom and a fat cap on top, these ribs can be commonly found as individual ribs also. Avoid the short ribs where there is a cross section of each bone, which is known as a flanken short rib. Remember to burp your EGG when opening at high temperatures and keep the dome closed when cooking.

Rub the ground spices along with the measured salt and pepper into the beef ribs or ox cheeks and leave to marinate for 1 hour at room temperature or overnight in the fridge.

Open your preheated EGG and place the beef ribs or ox cheeks into a preheated pan and sear until nicely browned all over, for 5–8 minutes. Remove.

Cook the onions and garlic in the dripping or oil in a cast iron pan or skillet for 10 minutes, until soft, then add all the remaining ingredients (except the hot sauce) and cook for 5 minutes, until the sauce thickens.

Add the beef to the sauce in the pan along with enough water to almost cover the beef. Cover, then cook in the EGG for about 1–1½ hours, until the beef is tender and falling apart (internal temperature of the meat should be about 93°C/199°F), topping up with water if it starts to dry out.

Remove the pan and discard the bay leaves and cinnamon stick. Cover and leave to rest for 20 minutes, then pull the meat into large chunks and stir back through the sauce to coat. Alternatively eat caveman style!

Adjust the seasoning to taste with salt and pepper and serve with hot sauce.

EGG SET UP
Indirect set-up;
the convEGGtor
in the legs-up
position with the
stainless steel
grid on top of the
convEGGtor legs.

TARGET TEMP
140–160°C/
275–320°F

SLOW ROAST CELERIAC 'JOINT'

Serves 4

1 large unpeeled celeriac (celery root), hairy roots discarded, scrubbed clean

4 tbsp olive oil

1 tsp flaky sea salt, plus extra for seasoning

Freshly ground black pepper

Flavoured butter, to baste (choose your own flavoured butter, but I favour a 'snail butter' that's traditionally served with French steaks, made by combining softened butter, crushed garlic, chopped parsley, finely chopped cured ham, chopped tarragon, freshly ground black pepper and a squeeze of lemon juice).

Until a few years ago, celeriac was a neglected vegetable. It's an ugly root, a bit rough to handle and, like the noble swede, was considered too much like hard work. But what chefs seem to have discovered recently is how useful it can be for grand dishes without meat. Celeriac is perhaps most impressive when roasted whole, but this recipe gives you the opportunity to present it to the table, carve it with due ceremony, then return the 'steaks' to the EGG to finish and crisp. Real table-side theatre. Remember to burp your EGG when opening at high temperatures and keep the dome closed when cooking.

Pierce the celeriac all over with a fork and then rub all over with 2 tablespoons of the olive oil and the measured flaky salt. Open your preheated EGG and cook the celeriac on the grill for a minimum of 2 hours, depending on the size of your celeriac, with the dome closed, basting it with your flavoured butter every 20 minutes or so, until the celeriac is browned and cooked through.

Remove the celeriac, then remove the convEGGtor and stainless steel grid with EGGmitts and grill gripper, replacing it with a cast-iron searing grid. Leave the celeriac to rest for 20 minutes, then cut into 3–4cm/1¼–1½in-thick steaks, brushing each cut side with the remaining olive oil and seasoning with salt and pepper.

Open the EGG and grill the steaks for 2–3 minutes on each side until lightly coloured, basting with the flavoured butter.

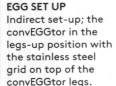

EGG SET UP
Indirect set-up; the convEGGtor in the legs-up position with the stainless steel grid on top of the convEGGtor legs.

Then...
Direct set-up with the stainless steel grid or cast-iron grid.

TARGET TEMP
140–160°C/275–320°F

Then...
200–220°C/400–425°F

BRAISED OR SALT-BAKED BEETROOT SALAD

Serves 4

For the braised or salted beetroots
8 small beetroots (beets)

To braise: 1 orange, cut in half,
6 whole, peeled garlic cloves,
4 bay leaves, salt

To salt-bake: coarse sea salt

For the salad
2 tbsp red wine or cider vinegar

2 tbsp olive oil, plus extra for drizzling

1 endive, thinly sliced

1 fennel bulb, core removed and very thinly sliced

100g/3½oz blue cheese, cut into small pieces

50g/½ cup walnuts, lightly toasted and roughly chopped

½ bunch of parsley, leaves picked and roughly chopped

Salt and freshly ground black pepper

It's odd that in the UK we regard beetroot mostly as a stainer of salads. Beetroot is a really useful vegetable, especially for fans of the EGG. It has a terrific, earthy flavour but also quite a lot of natural sugars, which seem to develop with long, slow roasting in an enclosed environment. The developed flavour is so good that in this case the root is cooked in the same way you'd cook meat, and then presented with a raw salad to complement it.

To braise the beetroots, wash and dry them, then place in a roasting pan or skillet with the orange halves, garlic cloves, bay leaves and some salt. Add 250ml/generous 1 cup of water and cook covered in foil in your preheated EGG, with the dome closed, for about 1 hour until tender. Cool, then peel and cut the beetroot in small dice. Throw away the orange halves, garlic and bay leaves.

To salt-bake the beetroot, spread 1cm/½in of coarse sea salt in a roasting pan. Wash the beetroots and, while still wet, roll them in the salt to coat. Arrange them in a single layer in the pan and cover tightly with foil, then burp and open the preheated EGG and roast the beetroots, with the dome closed, for about 1 hour until tender. Try to peel them while still warm, then cut into small dice.

Season the braised or salt-baked diced beetroot with salt, pepper, the vinegar and the 2 tablespoons of olive oil.

Spread the endive and fennel slices over a serving plate and drizzle with a little more olive oil, then top with the seasoned beetroot, the blue cheese, toasted walnuts and parsley.

EGG SET UP
Indirect set-up; the convEGGtor in the legs-up position with the stainless steel grid on top of the legs. You will need a skillet.

TARGET TEMP
180–200°C/
350–400°F

CREAM-FILLED BABY SQUASH

This might just be the most indulgent thing you can do with a vegetable. It works well with pumpkins or even butternut squash but it's also good with the little orange-fleshed summer squash, which seems happy to break down into the cheesy cream. The challenge in this dish is to take it to the point where the flesh is soft enough to scrape into with a spoon but without catastrophically losing integrity and collapsing. I've suggested serving it here with a refined dusting of grilled breadcrumbs; though, given half a chance, I prefer to go at it with big chunks of sourdough baguette.

Cut a lid out of each squash and scrape out the seeds. Season the insides of all the squash with salt, 1 tablespoon of the oil and ½ teaspoon of black pepper. Loosely return the lid to each, then burp and open your preheated EGG and cook for about 15–20 minutes, with the dome closed, until just about tender.

Meanwhile, cook the onions and garlic in 2 tablespoons of the oil in a large cast-iron pan for 5 minutes until softened, then add the sage and tomatoes and cook for 5 minutes. Add the cream and the cheeses, including the Parmesan, and stir until melted.

When the squash are almost cooked, burp the EGG, remove the lids and add some sauce to the middle of each, then roast without their lids (don't discard the lids) for a further 15–30 minutes, with the dome closed, until completely tender.

Burp the EGG and sprinkle the squash with the breadcrumbs (if using) and perhaps an extra grating of Parmesan over the top for the last 5 minutes.

Serves 6–8

6–8 baby squash

3 tbsp olive or sunflower oil

2 onions, roughly chopped

4 garlic cloves, roughly chopped

2 big sprigs of sage, leaves picked

2 tomatoes, roughly chopped

100ml/scant ½ cup double (heavy) cream

50g/scant 1 cup coarsely grated Parmesan cheese, plus (optional) extra to serve

150g/5½oz your favourite mixed melty cheeses (I love Taleggio and mozzarella, but I know quite honourable people who prefer a little blue cheese and some of the packaged 'fondue' mix you can pick up at the supermarket, or the sort of raclette that comes in a box)

Salt and freshly ground back pepper

6 tbsp breadcrumbs, fresh or dried, or a dirty great sourdough baguette, to serve

EGG SET UP
Indirect set-up; the convEGGtor in the legs-up position with the stainless steel grid on top of the convEGGtor legs.

TARGET TEMP
180–200°C/
325–400°F

CORN 'FONDANT'

Serves 4

4 corn on the cob, husks and silks removed, cobs cut into 2–3cm/¾–1¼in-thick slices

150g/⅔ cup butter, cut into slices

Pinch of sugar

250ml/generous 1 cup chicken stock or water

2 garlic cloves, crushed

1 tbsp chopped thyme leaves

A few chilli flakes (red pepper flakes)

Juice of 1 lemon

Salt and freshly ground black pepper

'Fondant' is a technique from extremely classical French cookery, usually used with potatoes. The idea is to poach the veg in a mixture of stock and butter, then, as the stock boils off, the now-cooked veg is fried in the remaining butter. You can do this with carrots, daikon radish, 'navet' turnips or even parsnips. Anything with a solid texture that you can trim into a 'drum' shape with a flat top and bottom. In this case, we're going to do it with thick slices of corn on the cob. The technique is fortuitously well suited to the EGG where you can combine heat underneath a skillet with an enclosed steaming environment. Remember to burp your EGG when opening at high temperatures and keep the dome closed when cooking.

Spread the corn slices over the base of a large roasting pan or skillet and top with the slices of butter, then season with salt and pepper and the pinch of sugar. Pour over enough stock or water to come halfway up the corn slices and cover with foil.

Open your preheated EGG and cook for 20 minutes with the dome closed until tender. Pull off the foil and cook for a further 5–10 minutes with the dome closed until the stock/water has all cooked off.

Stir through the garlic, thyme, chilli flakes and lemon juice, then cook on the EGG for another 5–10 minutes, basting with the flavoured butter mixture as you go, until the corn is beginning to colour a little.

EGG SET UP
Direct set-up with stainless steel grid

TARGET TEMP
150–180°C/
300–350°F

CHOCOLATE GRILLED SANDWICHES

There's no way round this. A grilled cheese sandwich is the best food in the world. Grubby, greedy, indulgent, bad for you and probably illegal in most civilized jurisdictions. Surely there could be nothing more fundamentally immoral? Wrong! This recipe has all the above advantages of a filthy grilled cheese. It's glorious and I'm damned if I'm going to apologize for it. I keep the ingredients for this in the back of the larder and if a few hardcore guests are still at the table when the rest have gone, it's time to whip out the gear and knock up a round of these. I have no idea why they go so well with both Sauternes and cheap tequila, but they do.

Use the Big Green Egg burger press to achieve the perfect weighted sear; if you don't have one, a cast iron skillet will do just fine.

Serves 4

8 slices of brioche (white sliced bread will also work if you have no shame)

3 tbsp melted butter

2 tbsp icing sugar (confectioners' sugar), for dusting the brioche

200g/7oz dark chocolate, coarsely grated

Big pinch of flaky sea salt

To serve
Whipped cream (flavoured with your favourite booze, if desired), or fruity olive oil

EGG SET UP
Direct set-up with stainless steel grid and a cast-iron plancha on top. If cooking for the feast you can cook it indirect.

TARGET TEMP
150–180°C/300–350°F

Brush the slices of brioche (or bread) on one side with melted butter and dust with some of the icing sugar. Lay out four slices with the non-dusted side up.

Top these slices with the grated chocolate and sprinkle with the flaky salt, then top with the remaining slices of brioche (or bread), with the dusted-side facing up.

Burp and open your preheated EGG and briefly grill the sandwiches in the EGG for about 45 seconds on each side, flipping them over carefully. Leave to rest for a minute or so, and then dust with more icing sugar.

Serve topped with whipped cream, perhaps flavoured with your favourite booze, or serve drizzled with fruity olive oil.

FAMILY GATHERINGS

Today, when families are so often spread across different cities, countries and even continents, it has never been more important to get together for celebrations. There's nothing more magical than picking up a brother from the airport, a sister arriving with the kids, Mum and Dad happy at the head of the table, and a kind of indistinguishable scrum of small cousins and pets getting under everyone's feet.

It doesn't have to necessarily be a religious festival, but the big, sit-down-at-the-table meal feels enormously significant, no matter what time of the year it falls. And the big table needs big, celebratory centrepieces. I doubt anyone will be planning to cook a whole fish and a turkey and a ham, but any one of these would be worth getting out the best crockery and cutlery for and ironing a tablecloth, and would a bunch of fresh flowers and some candles be too much to ask? Well, whatever you do, sit up straight, be nice to your siblings and don't talk back to your mum.

SERVES 10–14

FEAST MENU

WHOLE GRILLED HAKE:
30–45 minutes cooking time
(including the chimichurri)
180-200°C/350–400°F

SALT CARAMEL BAKED HAM:
4–6 hours cooking time
110-130°C/225–265°F

ROAST TURKEY LEG:
1½–2½ hours cooking time
110-130°C/225–265°F
then 180-200°C/350–400°F

TURKEY CROWN: 1½–2 hours
cooking time 180°C/350°F

STUFFING: 45 minutes cooking time
170–200°C/325–400°F

PURPLE-SPROUTING BROCCOLI:
4–6 minutes cooking time
180°C/350°F

ROAST POTATOES:
40–50 minutes cooking time
180°C/350°F

EGG FEAST SET UP
(if cooking everything together as a feast)

Load and light your EGG. Bring it to 180°C/350°F and add the convEGGtor basket with the convEGGtor in the legs-up position, the full stainless steel grid and multi-level grid.

FEAST METHOD
(if cooking everything together as a feast)

1 Cook the ham the day before or on the day and keep warm.

2 Make the chimichurri for the hake.

3 Cook the turkey legs. Cook the crown.

4 Cook the stuffing on the multi-level grid.

5 Remove the turkey to rest.

6 Cook the roast potatoes.

7 Cook the hake and the broccoli.

NOTE
Like with any other large family gathering, get as much prep done as you can before the big day; cook the ham, prepare the stuffing and peel the spuds.

WHOLE GRILLED HAKE WITH RED AND GREEN CHIMICHURRI

A big grilled fish, complete with head and tail, is a superb statement centrepiece for a feast, and the hake – a fish so good when caught in British waters that we ship almost all of them to Spain – is one of the most impressive to use. You can, if you wish, have your fishmonger remove the fillets from it in the usual way, then grill both, and serve side-by-side with the two 'chimis', but I prefer to make two deep cuts in the whole fish, one on each side of the backbone, creating two pockets for the sauces. It looks incredible as it comes to the table and it's still possible to serve boneless pieces with a choice of sauces. Remember to burp your EGG when cooking at high temperatures.

Make the green chimichurri sauce (see page 149). To make the red chimichurri, wrap the whole garlic head in a sheet of foil brushed with olive oil. Open your preheated EGG and roast for about 20–30 minutes, with the dome closed, until soft and sweet, then squeeze the flesh out of the papery skin and leave to cool.

Dirty cook the red (bell) peppers directly on the coals for more smoky flavours for about 20 minutes with the dome closed until softened and charred, turning occasionally keeping close to the lit part of the charcoal. When the peppers are cooked, remove from the EGG, cool slightly, then peel them, remove the stems and seeds, finely chop the peppers and place in a bowl with the garlic flesh. Blend together with everything else until smooth, adding salt and pepper to taste, and more vinegar to balance, plus more oil if necessary to loosen the consistency.

For the fish, arrange the hake in a decorative fashion on a baking tray or in a large skillet and season with salt and pepper. Depending on how you've chosen to handle your fish, either paint each fillet with a different chimichurri, green on one and red on the other, then spoon about 3 tablespoons more of each sauce over, or, fill the pockets on either side of the backbone with the two sauces. Open the EGG and roast, uncovered, for 10–15 minutes until just cooked through, with the dome closed but basting the fillets with the sauce a couple of times.

Serve the baked hake topped with any remaining chimichurri.

Serves 6

1 whole hake, about 1.5–2kg/ 3lb 5oz–4lb 8oz, butterflied, with head on if you prefer

Salt and freshly ground black pepper

For the green chimichurri
See salsa chimichurri (see page 149)

For the red chimichurri
1 head of garlic

2 red (bell) peppers

2 tbsp red wine vinegar

2 tsp smoked paprika

Small bunch of parsley, chopped

70ml/5 tbsp olive oil, plus extra for brushing

EGG SET UP
Indirect set-up; the convEGGtor in the legs-up position with the stainless steel grid on top of the convEGGtor legs.

TARGET TEMP
180–200°C/ 350–400°F

SALT CARAMEL BAKED HAM

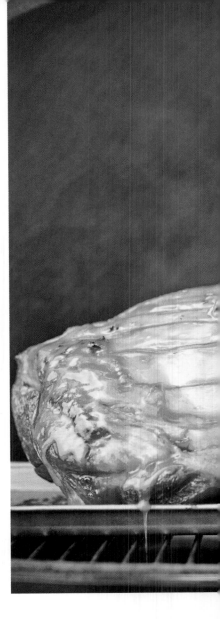

The EGG is the ideal place to cook your celebration ham. You can keep the temperature low for juiciness and texture, but the enclosing dome means you can build an incredibly impressive crust by continuous basting. The usual routine is for the butcher to cross-hatch the skin for a prettier presentation but that means the glaze slides off more easily. Instead, cut the lines yourself, horizontally. It's the same principal as farmers terracing fields around the contour lines, to 'prevent run-off' at all costs.

The glaze combines the superbly sticky syrup that's used by baristas to flavour coffee, with a little soy to darken it. The heat in the English mustard will cook out quickly, leaving a deep umami flavour, and remember to use the salt liberally.

Serves 12 + leftovers

1 unsmoked ham (with skin on), approx 4–5kg/8lb 13oz–11lb

1 small bottle (70cl/24oz) of caramel syrup from your favourite coffee shop

2 tsp English mustard powder

2 tbsp dark soy sauce

Salt and freshly ground black pepper

EGG SET UP
Indirect set-up; the convEGGtor in the legs-up position with the stainless steel grid on top of the convEGGtor legs.

TARGET TEMP
110–130°C/225–265°F

Decide which way your ham is going to sit when it's finished and, using a tough craft knife, cut horizontal scores into the skin.

Burp and open your preheated EGG and place the ham on the grill with the scored-skin facing down and cook with the dome closed for about 4–6 hours or until the internal temperature reaches 72°C/162°F (allow approximately 1 hour cooking time per 1kg/2lb 4oz).

When the ham goes in, prepare the glaze – mix all the remaining ingredients together in a bowl and set aside.

After 2 hours of cooking, start glazing the ham by brushing it with the glaze every 20 minutes until it begins to caramelize on the outside.

After 3½ hours of cooking, move the ham to a roasting tray or a triple layer of foil and pour the remaining glaze over, using a spoon or brush to glaze the ham until it has a lovely coloured sticky glaze. Continue to cook until the correct core temperature is reached.

Remove from the EGG and rest for at least 30 minutes before slicing thinly to serve warm, although it is also fantastic cold.

EGG ROAST TURKEY

The celebration turkey is the annual ingenuity test for the EGG master and the bar is set high. There's a lot at risk. The legs of a turkey are full of muscle, connective tissue and some amazing flavours. The breast, on the other hand, is delicate and requires careful handling to retain juiciness. There are dozens of opinions on how this can be best achieved on different sizes of bird, ranging from brining and low/slow cooking to elaborate tricks with foil. I'm a simple soul, so I just separate the legs from the crown of the bird, cook them both beautifully and then reassemble the bird to serve it.

To prepare your bird, remove the giblets and save for stock and gravy. Separate the turkey's legs at the hip joint. If you're sufficiently competent with a knife, you'll be able to leave the 'oysters' attached to the legs. If not, you can ask your butcher to do it for you. Pre-cook the legs and finish them alongside the crown.

TURKEY LEGS

2 tbsp vegetable oil
2 garlic cloves, finely chopped
1 tbsp finely chopped thyme
1 tsp salt
½ tsp coarsely ground black pepper
2 turkey legs

For the baste
50ml/scant ¼ cup white wine
10g/¼oz English mustard
1 tsp honey

EGG SET UP
Indirect set-up; the convEGGtor in the legs-up position with the stainless steel grid on top of the convEGGtor legs.

TARGET TEMP
110–130°C/225–265°F, then 170–200°C/325–400°F (The first temperature is the roasting phase, the second is to colour the legs a bit after resting and just before serving.)

Mix the oil, garlic, thyme, salt and pepper together, then rub this all over the turkey legs. Place the legs in a roasting tin and leave to marinate in the fridge for at least 1 hour but overnight is best.

Burp and open your preheated EGG and transfer the roasting tin to the EGG and roast for 1½–2½ hours, with the dome closed, until the meat is tender, but not falling apart. Meanwhile, mix the baste ingredients together in a small bowl and set aside.

After 1 hour, burp the EGG and pour the baste into the bottom of the roasting tin, and baste every 20 minutes until the legs are tender (internal temp for the legs should be about 75°C/167°F). Remove from the EGG and leave them to rest for 20 minutes.

Brush the turkey legs with a little of the baste and then crisp up the legs, skin-side down first, on the grill with the dome closed, for 2–5 minutes on each side until sticky and beginning to char. Serve with the roast turkey crown (see overleaf).

Serves 8–10

For the turkey crown

60g/2¼oz coarse salt

300ml/generous 1¼ cups
boiling water

2 tbsp black peppercorns

3 garlic cloves, crushed

2 tbsp chopped thyme leaves

2 bay leaves

1 turkey crown, about 3–4kg/
6lb 8oz–8lb 13oz

For the stuffing

1 onion, finely chopped

4 celery sticks, finely chopped

20g/1½ tbsp butter

2 tbsp olive oil

200g/7oz peeled cooked chestnuts,
finely chopped

300g/10½oz squash, peeled,
deseeded and coarsely grated

2 tsp finely chopped thyme,
rosemary or sage leaves

80g/1½ cups soft fresh breadcrumbs

1 egg

Salt and freshly ground black pepper

EGG SET UP
Indirect set-up; the
convEGGtor in the
legs-up position
with the stainless
steel grid or cast-
iron grid on top of
the convEGGtor
legs, or pizza stone
in place.

TARGET TEMP
180–200°C/350–
400°F (turkey
crown)
170–200°C/325–
400°F (stuffing)

TURKEY CROWN

For the brine, mix the salt with the boiling water in a jug until
the salt is dissolved, add all the flavourings, then add 300ml/
generous 1¼ cups of cold water and leave to cool.

Brine the turkey crown: place the crown in a deep dish, pour
over the brine mixture and leave to brine for 20–30 minutes in
the fridge.

Remove the crown from the brine and pat dry. Burp the EGG
and place the crown directly on the grill (or in a roasting dish),
breast-side up. Roast for 1½–2 hours, with the dome closed,
until the skin is crisp and golden brown and the meat is cooked
through (the internal temperature should be 74°C/165°F).

Burp the EGG and transfer the roast crown to a large plate and
let it rest for about 20 minutes before serving. To serve, use two
large metal skewers crossed to support the legs, put the roast
turkey legs in position and then lower the roast turkey crown
into position between them. Carve and serve with all the
accompaniments.

STUFFING

Fry the onion and celery in the butter and olive oil in a large
pan for about 15 minutes until golden brown and soft, adding
the chestnuts and squash for the last 5 minutes. Add the
chopped herbs, breadcrumbs and egg, season with salt and
pepper and mix well.

Roll the mixture into 12 individual stuffing balls, about walnut
sized, and place in a roasting tray. Burp and open the EGG
and cook the balls for the last 30 minutes alongside the
roasting crown.

PURPLE SPROUTING BROCCOLI

Purple sprouting broccoli is an absolute delight to eat. You've got to love a vegetable that comes with its own handle. It's also a quite robust little character, not delicate or hard to cook. And the best part is that, if the extremities get a little scorched, so much the better. Brassicas are immensely improved by a little fashionable carbonisation.

Toss all the ingredients together in a bowl, apart from the lemon juice, coating everything in the oil.

Burp and open the preheated EGG and grill in a single layer either straight on the grill or in the Big Green Egg perforated tray for about 2–3 minutes on each side, turning once, until the broccoli starts to colour and still has some bite.

Drizzle with a bit more olive oil, squeeze over the lemon juice and adjust the seasoning.

Serves 4

600g purple sprouting broccoli, separated into single stems

2 large shallots, thinly sliced (optional)

3 garlic cloves, crushed

30ml/2 tbsp olive oil, plus extra for drizzling

Finely grated zest and juice of ½ lemon

Salt and freshly ground black pepper

EGG SET UP
Direct set-up with stainless steel grid or cast-iron grid. Indirect if cooking for the feast.

TARGET TEMP
180–200°C/ 350–400°F

EGG ROAST POTATOES

Serves 4–6

1kg/2lb 4oz floury potatoes

Hot water, to cover

2 garlic cloves, left whole but peeled

50ml/scant ¼ cup olive oil

70g/5 tbsp salted butter

3 tbsp chopped fresh thyme
or rosemary

Flaky sea salt

Roast potatoes don't just complement celebratory feasts, they are secretly the most important part. Getting your potato game 'on point' will eventually be your defining talent as an EGG cook. There are many methods, but this one is a slightly less elegant version of the 'fondant' technique on page 204, an EGG-perfect combination of steaming and frying that should produce a cloud-like fluffy interior with a crisp and irresistible casing. Remember to burp your EGG when opening at high temperatures and keep the dome closed when cooking.

Peel the potatoes and cut or snap them into chunks. Open the preheated EGG and place the potatoes in a wide, shallow pan (the Big Green Egg paella pan is brilliant) on the grill.

Add hot water halfway up the potato chunks. As the water begins to simmer, add the garlic, olive oil and butter.

Cook for 10 minutes, then check the potatoes. Roll them all and top the water up if necessary. Cook for another 10 minutes.

The water should now have cooked off, leaving the potatoes steamed and lying in a pool of hot fat. Gently shuggle the pan around, making sure the potatoes are completely coated in fat. Splash over some more oil if you think it's necessary.

Move the pan to a cooler part of the EGG and continue to cook. Check regularly to see that they are getting evenly cooked. Test with a skewer. When they are crisp on the outside and tender within. Add the herbs and salt them enthusiastically and serve.

EGG SET UP
Indirect set-up; the convEGGtor in the legs-up position with the stainless steel grid on top of the convEGGtor legs. You will need a drip pan or skillet.

TARGET TEMP
180–200°C/350–400°F

JUST OUTSIDE THE BACK DOOR

There are many reasons I love my EGGs, but chief among them is where I've got them situated, just outside the back door. I don't know of any other grill kit that you can fire up in minutes, cook with quickly and without fuss and then shut down safely. It makes possible an entirely unique kind of cooking whereby, even in the depths of winter (if you keep a big 'hoodie' hanging next to the door) you can include something spectacularly fire-cooked in an indoor family meal, or even when just two of you are eating – truly the most minimal version, but because the EGG creates the occasion, no less of a feast.

These dishes don't come with an overall egg set-up, planning strategy or prep schedule. They are smaller, more individual affairs, but centrepieces nonetheless, around which you can size up or down and build your own feast.

RECIPES

BAKED CHICKEN
45-55 minutes cooking time 170–200°C/325–400°F

SMOKY SLOW BRISKET WITH WASABI CREAM
7-10 hours cooking time 110–120°C/225–250°F

CLAYPOT GLASS NOODLES WITH 'MAPO MINCE'
10-15 minutes cooking time 200–220°C/400–425°F

SARDINE LAYER BAKE
35-40 minutes cooking time 170–190°C/325–375°F

'MILK-FED' LAMB CHOPS
3-4 minutes cooking time 180–200°C/350–400°F

M'ROUZIA
2h 15 minutes cooking time 140–160°C/275–320°F

GRILLED SPATCHCOCK QUAILS WITH SAFFRON AÏOLI
10-12 minutes cooking time 180–200°C/350–400°F

GRILLED SOLE
5-10 minutes cooking time 200–220°C/400–425°F

CHICKEN YAKITORI
Various timings

WHAT MAKES AN OCCASION

It often feels like people of my culture, the Brits, are not great givers of feasts. Perhaps it's because our country is cold, our houses are compact, or perhaps, like so much in our history, we've weighed it down with too many class signifiers, so it feels impossible to truly relax at a formal meal. Whatever the reason, we food writers, in particular, have been openly jealous of almost everyone else. Why don't we get together for Seder every Friday? Why don't we celebrate weddings in a five-day orgy of eating and dancing? Why do I never seem to have the need for a 'Lazy Susan' at any of my family get-togethers?

It's perhaps no surprise, then, that we've embraced outdoor eating with quite such alacrity. God knows it's still too cold to stick your nose outside for at least four months of the year, and yet we've co-opted the idea, largely from the Americans and Australians, of outdoor cooking as a social event and we're seriously going for it. And why not? It encourages informality and relaxation, and it's lubricated with plenty of booze. But beneath that joyful, rambunctuous surface lurks something else – in fact, something rather lovely.

I've always felt that the best place to watch a party is from the cook's point of view. Lightly occupied with your duties, you can sniff out the gossip in the air, watch the old folks playing with babies, the older kids trying out their personas in a less judgemental playground and, as the evening goes on, men actually talking to each other about stuff other than sport. If I'm completely honest, the warm feeling that you've created all this, that you've made a space in which this can happen is the very best part. You've made all those lovely interactions occur. You've created an occasion.

I know. I'm a big bloke who grills meat and I shouldn't be talking like some kind of half-baked therapist, but here's the thing. Getting food on the table for people is all well and good, but it's what we do three times a day to survive. The key thing about an occasion is enabling the emotional intersection with eating and socializing that makes the moment live on in the memory. What we cook is important, but if we do the job right, an occasion is remembered in its entirety.

You can build an occasion around a wedding or a funeral, a reunion or a bar mitzvah, you can build it around a group of friends, a sports event, fireworks, a hot tub, a day at the beach, a hungover breakfast or a date. Hell, you can hire a marquee, lasers and a bouncy castle if that's what floats your boat, but those events are easy to forget if the magic isn't there. When the emotional connection is made... everything stays with you.

It's written into most world religions that there's a responsibility to take in, shelter and feed the traveller. At the same time, there are dire strictures on the guest not to break the implied contract. Historically, wars have broken out over breaches of hospitality, and ancient legends are full of tales of the horrible consequences. Perhaps, in an industrialized world, with families more widely distributed and digital connections more easily made than physical ones, it's easy to forget that the expression of hospitality is wired deep within us all. When we invite each other into our homes, we are effectively taking responsibility for making someone else feel great. To be a guest under those circumstances warms something entirely elemental inside us.

That's the place we need to reach. To make people feel warm, looked after, safe, protected and nourished. And if they feel that way, we feel terrific, because inside all of us there's a part that wants to look after others. It may be buried pretty deep in some cases... but it's in there, and sometimes it just takes a few friends, a few beers and some food on the EGG to reach it.

It might be the most important thing to remember that people have given you a great burden of trust. They are putting themselves in your hands. Yes, we need to feed them, but we must also ensure that everything else is ready for them to have the best of times and nothing can get in the way. Are people going to enjoy eating this, are they going to have a good time?

With this in mind, it's easier to understand what makes an occasion. It's not about size. It can be an occasion with 300 people or just two. It's not about expense or luxury, though those are always nice to have. It's not even primarily about the food. We make the occasion by imbuing an event with emotion... and we do that through old-fashioned hospitality.

What does that mean for us as hosts? To provide good food in comfortable surroundings. To be present and focused on the needs of our guests. It sounds like a tall order, like some type of terrifying multi-tasking, but it really isn't. Plan well, shop well. Have the best ingredients you can afford and good recipes. Be prepared, confident and relaxed. We can handle all those things if we take it easy, step-by-step, as we've tried to do in these recipes. If all this is done, there's only one thing left to do and that's to be a Charming Devil on the day. And that, I'm afraid, is ultimately down to you.

BAKED CHICKEN

Serves 4

8 smallish chicken thighs on the bone, skin on

2 onions, coarsely grated

1 x 400g/14oz can tomatoes, strained

2 preserved lemons, flesh removed and skin and pith finely chopped

1 cinnamon stick (or use ½ tsp ground cinnamon)

1 tsp ground ginger

1 tbsp ras al hanout

Pinch of saffron strands

50ml/scant ¼ cup olive oil

2 tbsp pomegranate molasses

Salt and freshly ground black pepper

This method of baking chicken is common across North Africa. Everything, meat and sauce ingredients, goes in together raw, and everything is cooked slowly, taking advantage of the EGG's controllability at low temperatures. Meat and vegetables flavour each other during the process, and towards the end of cooking, the surface tends to dry out a little and form a spectacularly delicious crust. This is one to set up and leave alone in the EGG. The less it's disturbed, fiddled with and peaked at, the better.

Season the chicken thighs with salt and pepper.

Mix the onions, tomatoes and preserved lemons in a large shallow pan. Mix in the remaining ingredients, seasoning with salt and pepper.

Bury the chicken pieces in the pulp, burp and open your preheated EGG, then bake for 45–55 minutes with the dome closed until the chicken is cooked through and the top is a bit scorched.

EGG SET UP
Indirect set-up; the convEGGtor in the legs-up position with the stainless steel grid on top of the convEGGtor legs. You will also need a drip pan, skillet or roasting pan.

TARGET TEMP
170–200°C/325–400°F

SMOKY SLOW BRISKET WITH WASABI CREAM

Serves 4–6

2kg/4lb 8oz brisket

For the rub

25g/1oz salt

25g/1oz sugar

15g/½oz smoked paprika

15g/½oz cayenne pepper

15g/½oz English mustard powder

10g/¼oz garlic powder

Pinch of allspice

Hickory smoking chunks

For the wasabi cream

75g/2½oz soured (sour) cream

About 25g/1oz pre-made wasabi paste

About 5g/⅛oz pre-made Japanese mustard

Honey, to taste

This is not a classic competition BBQ recipe for brisket, but a good, foolproof method for soft and smoky brisket. It's a game changer. We're not fussed about smoke rings and bark here, just a cracking sandwich, so this is a simpler approach that will please all but the purists.

The sauce, I know, sounds wrong, and you'd be quite justified in just reaching for your favourite old BBQ sauce. But please, give this one a go. Big Green Egg Note: The majority of British brisket tends to be less fatty than the US-grade beef. This is because US cattle are largely fed a grain diet whereas British are fed on pasture. The US meat will lay more fat on, which will keep the meat from drying out. Make sure you either invest in US-grade brisket or ensure the British beef you choose has as much fat on it as possible. Ask a good butcher for packer brisket, which is the American cut of brisket.

Ask your butcher to leave as much of the fat 'cap' as possible on top of the brisket. It's soft-textured stuff and, if we remember to keep the brisket 'right side up' throughout, it will melt during the slow cooking and automatically baste the meat.

Score into the fat with a sharp knife. Don't overdo it but you need a few places where the rub can get through to the meat. Combine all the dry ingredients for the rub in a bowl, then rub them thickly all over the surface of the meat.

Put the meat, along with any leftover rub, in a resealable plastic food bag and refrigerate overnight. If you remember, it's a good thing to go and visit it just before you go to bed and give it a bit of a roll around.

This is going to sound like terrible grill-heresy, but don't bother taking the brisket out of the fridge hours before cooking to 'come up to room temperature'. Meat that's cold at the cure takes longer to cook, which is exactly what we're trying to achieve.

Remove the brisket from the food bag and place it in a suitable roasting tray, pouring any juices over it. There are three phases to the cooking. First smoke the meat in the preheated EGG for

EGG SET UP

Indirect set-up; the convEGGtor in the legs-up position with the stainless steel grid on top of the convEGGtor legs.

TARGET TEMP

110–120°C/ 225–250°F

continued overleaf...

around 1½ hours. The roasting tray will catch any juices, so spoon these back over the top. Add hickory smoking chunks to the fire (these need to be added before the convEGGtor, brisket and stainless steel grid goes in). This will build up the dark, flavourful aromatic compounds, the bark, on the surface of the meat. Smoke for a further 1½ hours.

After 3 hours, burp the EGG, remove the meat and set aside, make sure you close your dome here as you want the EGG temperature to stay the same. Wrap the meat in butcher's paper and continue to cook. It's better to cook to temperature not time, so smoke probably for at least another 4–7 hours until the core temperature reaches 95°C/203°F.

Burp and remove the brisket from the EGG and leave it to rest, still wrapped in the paper, for at least 30 minutes before slicing and serving.

For the wasabi cream, start with the soured cream in a bowl and add the wasabi paste, tasting as you go. Don't bother with the expensive wasabi – the stuff in squeezy plastic tubes is plenty good enough for this rather blasphemous combination. Stop adding the wasabi while you're still well short of face-burningly hot.

Now add some of the Japanese mustard (also the plastic tube stuff... it's brilliant). Just a little of this stuff goes a very long way, so go carefully until you have enough heat to just prickle in the nose, then add just enough honey to take the edge off. Personally, I don't like too much sweetness, and how you season your own will probably vary with the sweetness of your brisket rub. Serve the wasabi cream with the sliced brisket.

CLAYPOT GLASS NOODLES WITH 'MAPO MINCE'

Mapo tofu has become an international classic, served in Chinese restaurants all over the world. The numbing spice effect of the Szechuan peppercorns is brilliantly transported around the mouth by all that amazingly flavoured oil and it has the ability to flavour anything added to it. It's perhaps not a common home-cooked dish in the West because, for the best results, mapo tofu must be stir-fried in a wok.

To run a wok properly, you either need a) a fully equipped Chinese restaurant kitchen with extra hot gas jets, b) a surplus Pratt & Whitney F100 turbofan engine from an F-16 with the afterburner turned upwards, or c) a Big Green Egg. In short, you need heat.

I've come across some really interesting variations on mapo tofu, including beef or venison versions, which were excellent and provided many laudable attempts to avoid tofu. I've had it with cubes of butternut squash, carrot, celeriac or just potato, and on one occasion in Italy, a very creditable 'Ma Po Melanzane'.

I make the mince in large batches whenever I have the EGG/wok combination fired up. Once it's cooked and cooled, I cut it into cubes and freeze it. If I'm feeling very classical about it, I can then use it to flavour a batch of silken tofu cubes, but I'm going to be brutally honest here, it's also extraordinarily good microwaved and poured into a toasted pitta when you have a sufficient hangover.

In this recipe, it's served with glass noodles (aka bean noodles, mung bean vermicelli, dangmyeon, haifun or harusame), using a clay pot to help the flavours combine.

Remember to burp your EGG when opening at high temperatures and keep the dome closed when cooking.

Serves 4

Pinch of Szechuan peppercorns

2 tbsp vegetable oil, plus extra for frying the eggs

15g/½oz peeled garlic cloves, grated

15g/½oz peeled fresh ginger, grated

2 red chillies, deseeded and finely chopped

225g/8oz minced (ground) pork

30g/1oz doubanjiang (Szechuan spicy fermented bean paste)

2 tbsp dark soy sauce

4 tbsp chicken stock

15g/½oz cornflour (cornstarch)

2 tsp sesame oil, plus extra for the clay pot

1 x 250g/9oz packet dried glass noodles

Boiling water, to soak the noodles

2 large eggs

15g/½oz Japanese red pickled ginger (beni shoga), drained

continued overleaf...

EGG SET UP
Direct set-up with the stainless steel grid, and the Big Green Egg wok. Or for a traditional set-up where the base of the wok and sides sit closer to the heat, sit the wok in the middle on the convEGGtor basket.

TARGET TEMP
200–220°C/400–425°F

Open your preheated EGG and fry the Szechuan peppercorns in the vegetable oil in the wok until they start to pop, then add the garlic, ginger and chillies. Allow them to soften for a few seconds.

Add the minced pork. It should start to give up its own fat fairly quickly. Keep the heat high and everything moving until the pork is browned and granular. If things are getting too hot at this stage, close the dome for 5–10 seconds; when you next open the EGG, burp and open the dome slowly.

Add the doubanjiang and stir until it's completely combined and the pork has gone red throughout. Now add the soy sauce and chicken stock and, to get a cooler temperature, close both vents so they are nearly shut but some air is still getting in so the dish can simmer for a few moments. Mix the cornflour into a slurry with 1 tablespoon of water, then stir it through the simmering pork so it thickens and becomes glossy. Take the wok off the heat and close the dome, stir in the sesame oil and leave to rest while you soak the noodles.

Soak the noodles in boiling water in a bowl. As they soften – usually around 5 minutes – ladle some of the oil from the pork into the bottom of your clay pot and warm it over the EGG. If you have been using your convEGGtor basket to cook on, now place your stainless steel grid on top before adding in your clay pot.

Drain the noodles, then toss them in the oil in the clay pot. Dollop the pork mixture on top, add an extra few drops of sesame oil and just a splash of hot water to start the flavours of the pork flowing down to the noodles and creating fragrant steam. Close the lid of the pot, burp your EGG and add the pot to the stainless steel grid to sit and simmer for a few minutes.

Alongside the clay pot, add in a small skillet or frying pan and fry the eggs in a little vegetable oil until cooked to your liking.

Serve the pork and noodles in the clay pot topped with the fried eggs and some red pickled ginger.

SARDINE LAYER BAKE

Serves 4

500g/1lb 2oz waxy potatoes, thinly sliced

350g/12oz Roma tomatoes, thinly sliced

2 garlic cloves, thinly sliced

4 tbsp olive oil

12 fresh sardines, gutted and scaled (you can used canned ones, too)

Finely grated zest and juice of 1 lemon

150g/5½oz stale sourdough bread, blended into coarse breadcrumbs

2 tsp fresh thyme leaves

Small bunch of parsley, chopped

Salt and freshly ground black pepper

This recipe combines elements of Swedish 'Jansson's Temptation' with Cornish Stargazy Pie and a traditional layered fish and potato bake from Tunisia. It's a superb combination of flavours, brought together when the oily fish melt a little in the gentle heat of the EGG.

Layer the potatoes on the bottom of a pie pan/dish 24cm (9½in) diameter and season with salt and pepper. Add a layer of the sliced tomatoes and garlic, then season with more salt and pepper and drizzle with 2 tablespoons of the olive oil.

Layer on the sardines, then squeeze over the lemon juice.

Mix the lemon zest, breadcrumbs, thyme and parsley together with the remaining olive oil, then scatter in an even layer over the top.

Burp and open your preheated EGG and bake, uncovered, for 35–40 minutes, with the dome closed, until cooked through.

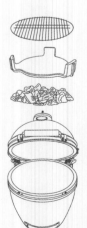

EGG SET UP
Indirect set-up; the convEGGtor in the legs-up position with the stainless steel grid on top of the convEGGtor legs.

TARGET TEMP
170–190°C/325–375°F

'MILK-FED' LAMB CHOPS

Serves 4–6

12 small 'frenched' lamb chops
250g/9oz buttermilk
Large pinch of salt

For the anchoïade
2 garlic cloves, finely chopped
1 sprig of rosemary, leaves picked
and finely chopped
1 sprig of thyme, leaves picked
and finely chopped
150g/5½oz pitted black olives
6 anchovy fillets canned in oil
Finely grated zest of ½ lemon

In Spanish cookery, there's a tradition of grilling un-weaned lamb. I've tried it a few times and I have to confess I find the flesh tasteless and the texture worryingly insubstantial. Instead, I prefer to steal from the South Asian technique of marinating lamb in yoghurt or buttermilk. The lactic acid content does begin to break down the meat after a surprisingly short time, so perhaps it's better not to take it too far. You want some of the textural delicacy of the milk-fed stuff but to also retain properly developed flavour. In this case, we've gone with the Mediterranean anchoïade as a crust, which brings an anchovy flavour that's particularly good with lamb.

Put the chops in a shallow dish, pour over the buttermilk, add the large pinch of salt and leave to marinate for 30 minutes.

Meanwhile, blend all the anchoïade ingredients together into a smoothish purée.

Remove the chops from the marinade and dry them with paper towels, then paint the edges of each chop with some of the anchoïade. Place on a tray and leave, uncovered, in the fridge to dry out – this will take 1–4 hours. Keep the remaining anchoïade in the fridge.

Burp and open your preheated EGG and grill the chops for 3–4 minutes, with the dome closed, on each side until crisp, then serve topped with the remaining anchoïade.

EGG SET UP
Direct set-up with
the stainless steel
grid or cast-iron grid.

TARGET TEMP
180–200°C/350–400°F

M'ROUZIA

Serves 6–8

1kg/2lb 4oz lamb shoulder, diced

3 garlic cloves, crushed

15g/½oz ras el hanout

10g/¼oz Aleppo pepper

5g/⅛oz ground ginger

5g/⅛oz ground cinnamon

1 cinnamon stick

Pinch of saffron strands

15g/½oz salt

300g/generous 2 cups sultanas
(golden raisins)

100g/7 tbsp unsalted butter

2 onions, grated

100g/3½oz honey

100g/1¼ cups flaked (slivered)
almonds, toasted

Urban homes in Morocco often don't have a domestic oven. Cooks will assemble the ingredients of dinner in a tagine or casserole, tied up in a colourful identifying cloth, and drop it off at the bread bakery on the way to work. The bakers put the pots in the oven once the bread is finished and everything cooks throughout the day in the dying heat. In the evening, the next shift of bakers remove the pots and put them outside the bakery door to be picked up. This method is, of course, simple to replicate with the EGG, so here's the recipe for M'rouzia, which is the most intense, cooked-down lamb/fruit/nut combination. It's spectacularly deep and complex – though extremely un-photogenic – and a little goes a long way with rice, couscous or flatbreads.

Put the diced lamb in a non-metallic dish, add the garlic, ras el hanout, Aleppo pepper, ground ginger and cinnamon, saffron strands and salt, mix well, then cover and leave to marinate in the fridge overnight. Soak the sultanas in a bowl of water overnight.

Using the direct set-up, brown the marinated meat in the melted butter in a tagine in the preheated EGG for 3–5 minutes, then add the grated onions. Sweat for 5–10 minutes, with the dome closed, until softened, then drain (and reserve) the sultanas and add the sultana soaking water and the honey to the tagine.

Using the indirect set-up, cover the tagine and cook for an hour or so, with the dome closed, then stir in the sultanas and cook for another hour. Remove the tagine lid for the last 30 minutes to let the mixture dry out to a jammy consistency.

Serve, sprinkled with the toasted flaked almonds.

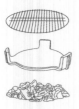

EGG SET UP
Direct set-up with the stainless steel grid or cast-iron grid.

Then...
Indirect set-up; the convEGGtor in the legs-up position with the stainless steel grid on top of the legs.

TARGET TEMP
140–160°C/275–320°F

GRILLED SPATCHCOCK QUAILS WITH SAFFRON AÏOLI

Serves 4

4 quails

Olive oil, for basting

Small bunch of fresh rosemary tied together to form a 'basting brush'

2 lemons, cut in half

Salt and freshly ground black pepper

I love interactive foods when lots of people are eating together. Along with plentiful booze, it's a phenomenal social lubricant that encourages even the most uptight guests to dive in and get greasy together. It's impossible to share quails and aïoli while maintaining decorum and without laughing joyfully at yourself and others.

Remove the backbones from the quails with a sturdy pair of scissors. Open out each bird and flatten it in position with two crossed wooden skewers, then season with salt and pepper.

Make the saffron aïoli (see oveleaf).

Burp and open your preheated EGG and grill the quails for 5–6 minutes, with the dome closed, on each side, regularly basting with olive oil using the herb 'basting brush', until cooked through with just a hint of pink. Grill the lemon halves, cut-side down, alongside the quails.

Burp, remove the grilled quails from the EGG and squeeze over the lemon juice. Leave to rest for 5 minutes before serving with the saffron aïoli.

EGG SET UP
Direct set-up with the stainless steel grid or cast-iron grid.

TARGET TEMP
180–200°C/
350–400°F

continued overleaf...

SAFFRON AÏOLI

It's difficult to know what to call this recipe. Aïoli and its variations are Spanish/Catalan/Provençal emulsion sauces of olive oil and garlic. The principle is the same as mayonnaise only the emulsifying ingredient is garlic rather than egg yolk and mustard. Here, we've roasted the garlic to give it a sweeter, more mellow and developed flavour, and then used both egg and a small amount of mustard to make the emulsification easier. Finally, it's flavoured with aromatic saffron and lemon. It's a terrible mashup but it tastes sublime.

Makes 300ml

1 head of garlic
Big pinch of saffron strands
1 tbsp warm water
2 large, free-range egg yolks
2 tsp Dijon mustard
200ml/scant 1 cup extra-virgin olive oil, plus extra for brushing
Juice of 1 lemon
Salt and freshly ground black pepper

Wrap the whole garlic head in a sheet of foil brushed with olive oil, then open and burp your preheated EGG and cook the garlic for about 20 minutes with the dome closed until soft. Squeeze the flesh out onto a plate and leave to cool.

Soak the saffron strands in the warm water for 10 minutes.

Whisk together the egg yolks, mustard, roast garlic flesh, saffron water, a big pinch of salt and a little black pepper in a bowl.

Pour the olive oil into a jug that is easy to pour from, then slowly start whisking a few drops of oil into the egg mix.

Slowly increase the quantity of oil added each time, whisking in each addition so it is properly amalgamated, before adding the next. Once the sauce has started to hold its shape, you can start to add the oil in a thin stream.

When you have added all the oil and the aïoli holds its shape, whisk in the lemon juice, taste and check the seasoning and add a little more salt. Cover and refrigerate if necessary.

GRILLED SOLE

A whole sole, one of the triumphs of old-school restaurant cooking, requires a 'salamander' – a type of professional grill that can provide strong heat from above for finishing gratins or steaks. The whole fish, which has had it's skin removed, is delicate and thin, so it requires fierce heat to brown the outside without overcooking and ruining the interior. A metal plate is usually used so some heat comes from below, but the fish shouldn't be 'flipped' while cooking. Outside of a professional kitchen, the EGG is the only appliance I know that can do this job. Remember to burp your EGG when opening at high temperatures and keep the dome closed when cooking.

Have your sole gutted and skinned by your fishmonger. Head on or off, it's up to you. Season the sole with salt and pepper.

Combine the capers, herbs or wild garlic, lemon zest and juice and vinegar in a small bowl. Set aside.

Place the Dover sole on an oiled flat baking tray or drip pan and cook in the preheated EGG, with the dome closed, basting it regularly with the olive oil and butter. The cooking time will depend on the thickness of your sole, but it will only be a matter of a few minutes. You'll know it's done if you use a sharp knife to cut carefully along the spine at the thickest part, look inside and see that it's just still ever so slightly translucent close to the bone, or a probe thermometer reads 63°C.

Dish up the fish onto a large serving plate, then add the caper and herb mixture into the remaining oil/butter in the baking tray, stir to combine and then pour over the fish.

Serves 2

1 large Dover sole, gutted and skinned (approximately 350g/12oz)

20g/¾oz salted capers, rinsed and roughly chopped

20g/¾oz fines herbes (equal amounts of chopped parsley, chives, tarragon and chervil), or wild garlic, finely chopped

Finely grated zest and juice of 1 lemon

1 tsp white wine vinegar

100ml/3½fl oz olive oil, plus extra for greasing

25g/1oz butter

Salt and freshly ground black pepper

EGG SET UP
Indirect set-up; the convEGGtor in the legs-up position with the stainless steel grid or cast-iron grid on top of the convEGGtor legs.

TARGET TEMP
200–220°C/
400–425°F

YAKITORI

Like many supposedly ancient Japanese cooking traditions, Yakitori appeared around 1900, during the Meiji Period when taboos against eating meat were collapsing under a westernizing Emperor. It was a popular street or snack food, which used excellent precision butchery to extract dozens of flavours and sensations from cheap chickens and simple charcoal grills.

Like the mangal tradition or souvlaki cooking, it requires a different approach to the grill. You don't heave in great chunks of meat, close the dome and pop a beer, you need to spend ages in preparation of tiny skewers and then kind of hunker down over the heat source, watching, fiddling, turning and basting so each different cut gets precisely the heat and attention it needs to shine.

There are a couple of dozen common skewers that crop up in every 'yakitori-ya' – or grill shop – ranging from simple pieces of fillet to diced tails, thyroid gland and skin. All are delicious, though some involve textures that might challenge the Western palate (crunchy knee cartilage anyone?). For the home cook, yakitori is complicated by mathematics. You need maybe four hearts for a single skewer and, unless you're going to get into some really quite involved genetic modification, the average chicken only has one.

A get-together around the EGG, therefore, is the ideal time to try yakitori, as you'll have the excuse to get a few birds in at once, the inclination to do the prep work and an audience with enough varied tastes that you might only need one or two of the more challenging types in your final selection.

PLANNING

You'll get a reasonable spread of skewers from three chickens – they would give you loads of simple breast/fillet skewers, for example, but a single heart one – so a good yakitori feast is going to require some advance planning. I usually buy whole chickens throughout the year for regular family 'leg and breast' portions, so I keep bags in the freezer into which I can 'collect' certain types of trim over several months. I save the hearts, livers and gizzards from the giblet bags. Before putting the carcass in the stockpot, I'll harvest the 'oysters', the tail and the triangular 'rib' flaps. All neatly filed away and safely frozen down, you soon build up a useful, if slightly disturbing, hoard of bits.

It's also worth talking to your butcher. The majority of the chicken they sell will be neatly trimmed breast so, with a bit of notice, they might well be able to amass a fairly large collection from what would otherwise go to waste. Your butcher's wholesaler will also have packs of hearts, livers, gizzards and maybe even necks that can usually be ordered with a little advance planning.

Let's look at butchering a single bird and you'll see what that produces. This will make more sense of the planning.

BUTCHERY

You'll need a small, sharp knife, a heavier knife or light cleaver, latex/disposable gloves, a chopping board to work on, and I usually spread out a tray or a large piece of greaseproof or butcher's paper on which I can arrange the pieces as I trim them.

STOCKPOT

Assuming we're starting with a standard bird, from a British butcher or supermarket, undo the trussing bands and remove the giblet bag. Separate out the heart, the liver, the gizzard and the neck.

1. Heart. Trim away any egregious tubes or pipework at the top, then slice about three-quarters of the way down one side of the heart and open it flat like a book. Use the tip of your finger or the back of the knife to scrape out any blood.

2. Liver. Trim away any membrane or ducts, and examine the liver carefully. If there are small bruised sections or areas that look faintly green, trim and discard. Don't be afraid, though, to toss the whole thing if it looks too battered. Livers are delicate and the butchery process rarely takes care of them.

3. Straighten the neck and feel carefully along its length. It's skinny and delicate but, like any other animal, a chicken uses good muscle to hold up its head. You should be able to identify two long, thin cylindrical muscles running either side of the 'spikes' at the back of the spine and two even skinnier ones along the 'throat' at the front. Run your knife along the bone to remove them. They will be tiny and you'll doubt they are worth the effort, but enough of them will make the most sublime skewer.

4. Cut the gizzard in half and peel off the tough outer membrane. Bones, blood and heart trim can go into the stockpot bowl and you'll start to see things lining up on your tray. I always find this bit the most satisfying... that I've already managed to extract interesting stuff and I haven't even started on what most cooks regard as 'the chicken' proper.

5. Articulate the hip joint to loosen it, then cut the leg off, through the hip joint.

6. Place the whole leg cut-side upwards, then, doing that thing that surgeons do of stretching the meat apart with thumb and forefinger, use your small knife to cut down to the bone and open up the entire leg. Now get the tip of the knife under the bone at the hip and slip it downwards, under the 'knee' and all the way to the other end. It gets easier once you've done it a few times, but don't worry if your cuts are initially short and choppy. Add the bone to the stockpot bowl.

7. Cut off the lower leg meat below the knee cartilage – let's call it 'shin' (though it isn't). Leave the skin on. Flatten out into a rough rectangle and place on your tray.

8. Cut the knee cartilage off the thigh meat. I usually look at it ruefully, wish I was braver, then add it to the stockpot. Remove the skin from the rest of the thigh and start a 'skin pile' on your tray. Cut the thigh meat into three pieces – if you look at the inside, there's an obvious line where you can separate a small from a large muscle, then you can cut the larger one across into two halves. Pile this onto the tray – we'll call it 'thigh'.

9. Chop the tail off. Remove the skin and gland, split the tail in half and place on the tray.

10. Trim off the wing. Cut out the web triangle of the wing and add it to your skin pile. Separate the thickest, upper part of the wing, open it up from the inside and cut out the bone. This is much the same way you treated the thigh, just more fiddly. Once the bone has been lifted out and added to the stockpot bowl, add the meat to the 'mince bowl'.

11. Slice along the rest of the bones and remove as much meat as you can. Add any meat you can recover to the mince bowl and add the bones to the stockpot bowl, and promise yourself that, in the future, you'll obsessively search online for the dozens of YouTube videos you'll need for proper wing butchery, or possibly consider taking a degree in veterinary surgery with a minor in avian physiology.

12. Remove the breasts, leaving the fillets on the carcass. Keep the skin in place. Cut off the triangular end point, then slice across into even-sized chunks. Add the trimmed skin to the stockpot bowl and any meat to the mince bowl. Place the breast pieces on your tray.

13. Remove the fillet. Trim out the tendon running through it. Add the tendon to the stockpot bowl and place the fillet on the tray.

14. Remove the oysters and place on the tray.

15. Looking at the side of the carcass, cut out the triangular sheet of muscle between the last ribs and the spine. This is referred to as 'rib' and can make a skewer all of its own, but in this case, add it to the skin pile on the tray.

16. With your small knife, remove every last scrap of meat that's left. Pieces you find up around the base of the neck and the wishbone can be added to the neck meat on the tray. Anything else can go into the mince bowl.

17. Everything that's left should go into the stockpot bowl.

SKEWERING

Skewering is a bit of an art form when cooking over fire, and yakitori is a good way to understand the principles. In some cooking methods, kofte would be a good example – a flat metal skewer is used to conduct heat into the heart of larger chunks of meat and effectively cook it from the inside as well as the outside. Yakitori is all about cooking small, delicate pieces of meat quickly, so they're crisp and well flavoured on the outside and stay moist and juicy inside.

The standard skewer for yakitori, called a kushi, is made of bamboo, which conducts no heat at all. The principle of yakitori butchering and the use of the kushi is to trim the pieces so they cook at similar speeds and to the best advantage of the meat. In some cases, the kushi is used to hold the most delicate cuts, tightly packed into a roll, so they cook with a crust but much of the meat inside is protected from the heat. In other cases, the skewering holds the meat out flat, creating a larger surface area and allowing the heat to penetrate tougher pieces.

Sometimes the skin is removed so flavours can penetrate, sometimes it's left on as a protective coat, a source of lubricating fat or just because it tastes phenomenal.

The method for skewering is usually to place the meat flat on a chopping board on the edge of the bench, to hold the meat in position with the fingers or palm of one hand and to carefully slide the kushi in from the side.

Once the skewer is loaded, with everything tightly in place, use a knife to trim up the edges so each piece is of similar cross section. Once you're cooking, you want to be able to control regular heat throughout each piece by turning it, so a certain neat symmetry really improves the results. Most importantly, all the trimmed material goes into the mince bowl.

THE MEATBALL

Weigh the meat in the mince bowl and then weigh out 10 per cent of the amount in panko breadcrumbs. Either put the meat through a mincer or chop it as finely as you can with a knife. Spread it on a plate and put it into the freezer for 20 minutes, then bring it out and chop it through again.

Add the breadcrumbs, then 20 per cent of the weight in onion that's been grated and squeezed quite dry. Season with salt and black pepper. Mix vigorously with a silicone spatula until the mixture starts to get sticky.

Taking a tablespoon of the mixture at a time in wet hands, roll into tight balls and drop each one into a pan of simmering water for about a minute. Scoop out and place them on paper towels to drain and then put them straight into the fridge until you are ready to cook.

THE TARE

Next to the grill in every yakitori-ya sits a large and ominous-looking jar, which contains the tare. Tare is the marinade/glaze/dip that makes yakitori irresistible. It contains a lot of the traditional Japanese flavourings, along with alcohol, chicken stock and enough sugar to promote both caramelization and glazing. The grill man dips the skewers into the tare pot before cooking and often goes back to it during the process. It may get painted onto some skewers, it may even feature as a dressing when they're served.

It's magical stuff. It's also, by tradition, never thrown away. That's right. All those dipped skewers add to the flavour which builds and improves over time, and even when a batch of new tare has to be made, old tare is added so the magic is passed on.

This is, perhaps, a little difficult for a cook who's just doing the occasional yakitori session rather than running a busy bar; it also contravenes food preparation regulations in most jurisdictions, so I strongly recommend you make fresh tare every time you cook and you won't be disappointed.

You need around 1L/4⅓ cups of tare in order to fill a narrow jug deep enough to dip a whole skewer. At the end of a cooking session, I bring the tare to a gentle simmer in a saucepan, top up the ingredients to 1L/4⅓ cups, then cool it in the fridge and freeze it. Before reusing it, I defrost and bring it back to a simmer before cooling and reusing. You should not do this.

Everyone's tare is their own business, but this would be a good starter recipe:

Roast your chicken carcass and the contents of your stockpot bowl, along with an onion, halved but not peeled, and a roughly chopped knob of fresh ginger in a roasting tin in a preheated oven at 220°C/425°F for 15 minutes; if you do this in an EGG, the smoky flavour adds an extra depth. Everything should be very deep brown.

Transfer everything to a stockpot and add half a bottle (75cl) of mirin. You'll also need to add a quarter of a bottle of sake, but use some of it to make sure every last bit is 'deglazed' out of the bottom of the roasting tin first. Just to complete the round, add a small bottle (350ml/12oz) of Japanese beer. Bring to a simmer and let the alcohol cook out a bit before adding about 500ml/ 2 cups soy sauce, 100g/½ cup of sugar, 100g/3½oz of honey and 50g/1¾oz of brown or white miso. A couple of dried, chopped shiitake mushrooms would definitely not go amiss.

Allow this mixture to simmer for around 30 minutes, then strain the tare into your dipping container, taste and adjust the seasoning. Leave to cool before using.

SETTING UP THE EGG

You'll need to set up your EGG so you can watch and manipulate the skewers while you cook and so the skewers are supported. I've found the easiest way to do this is to set up the EGG without the convEGGtor, running at a low–medium temperature and with everything prepared and set up on the bench. When you start, the dome will be open and the temperature will tend to rise.

Prepare a couple of house bricks by wrapping them each in several layers of foil. When you're ready to cook, close the bottom vents, lift the dome and place the two foil-covered bricks on the grill, on their edges and 15cm/6in apart. Work calmly but quickly and plan to cook in two or three 'waves', closing the dome and allowing the temperature to settle between cooking sessions.

SKEWER RECIPES

Heart (hatsu)
Three butterflied hearts per skewer. Dip repeatedly in the tare while grilling. Serve with shichimi togarashi.

Liver (reba)
Roll three pieces of liver tight onto each skewer. Grill fast and hot so it remains rare at the core. Dip in the tare at the end.

Neck (seseri)
'Stitch' the skewer back and forth through the strips of meat. Dip repeatedly in the tare while grilling. Serve with a soy dip.

Gizzard (sunagimo)
Three halves of gizzard per skewer. Cook slowly, dipping repeatedly in the tare during grilling to keep the temperature under control.

Shin and onion (torinegi)
Roll two pieces of shin, skin-side out, and alternate with lengths of spring onion (scallion). Paint with tare for the last few seconds of grilling. Serve with a small piece of fresh lemon.

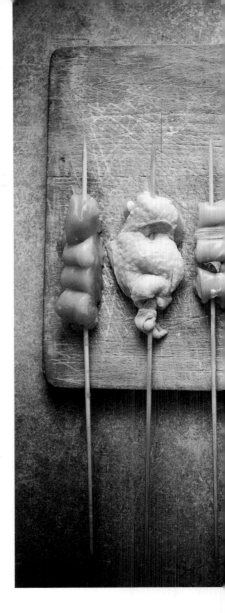

Thigh (momo)
Use two skewers to flatten out each piece. Grill the fat-side first to crisp, then flip to seal the underside.

Tail (bonjire)
Thread three pieces of tail onto each skewer. Dip repeatedly in the tare while cooking.

Skin (kawa)
'Stitch' skin tightly onto a skewer to create a narrow cylinder. Cook fast so the fat renders and sizzles. Serve with a scrunch of crystal sea salt.

Breast (mune)
Roll three pieces of breast tightly onto each skewer. Paint with soy sauce while grilling and serve with dabs of wasabi paste.

Fillet (sasami)
Thread a single skewer through the length of a single fillet. Grill fast with repeated dipping in the tare during cooking. Serve painted with tare.

Oysters (soriresu)
Three per skewer. Grill fast.

Meatball (tsukune)
Three per skewer. Grill gently, repeatedly painting with the tare to build up a glaze during cooking. Allow to char a little.

INDEX

Big Green Egg

The Big Green Egg is the original and the best ceramic grill and oven, beloved by Michelin kitchens around the globe. Based on the Japanese kamado oven, the Big Green Egg includes NASA-specification ceramics and a design so sturdy that it carries a lifetime warranty.

The Big Green Egg lets the home cook create fantastic restaurant-quality meals to share with friends and family. Fuelled only by natural lump wood charcoal, it creates flavours and textures like no other, whether on the grill, oven roasting, smoking, 'dirty' grilling direct on the coals or cooking low and slow. The Big Green Egg is equally amazing for cooking poultry, meat, seafood and vegetables; check out more delicious recipes and tips at www.biggreenegg.co.uk.

ABOUT THE AUTHOR

Tim Hayward writes for the *Financial Times* every week and is a panellist on BBC Radio 4's *The Kitchen Cabinet*. He won the Guild of Food Writers 'Food Journalist of the Year' in 2014, 2015 and 2022, and was the Fortnum and Mason Food Writer of the Year for 2014 and 2022. He is the author of *Food D.I.Y.*, *The DIY Cook*, *Knife*, *The Modern Kitchen*, *Loaf Story* and *Charcuterie from Scratch*.